Translation Stories from Modern China

Translation Stories from Modern China

Bonnie S. McDougall

Cambria Sinophone Translation Series
General Editor: Kyle Shernuk (Georgetown University)
Advisor: Christopher Lupke (University of Alberta)

Amherst, New York

For Anders and Torkel

Copyright 2024 Cambria Press

All rights reserved.
Printed in the United States of America

No part of this publication may be reproduced, stored in or introduced into a retrieval system, or transmitted, in any form, or by any means (electronic, mechanical, photocopying, recording, or otherwise), without the prior permission of the publisher.

Requests for permission should be directed to permissions@cambriapress.com, or mailed to:
Cambria Press
100 Corporate Parkway, Suite 128
Amherst, New York 14226, USA

Library of Congress Cataloging-in-Publication Data

Names: McDougall, Bonnie S., 1941- author.

Title: Translation stories from modern China / Bonnie S. McDougall.

Description: Amherst, New York : Cambria Press, 2024. | Series: Cambria Sinophone translation series | Includes bibliographical references. | Summary: "This book could be called the autobiography of a translator: it describes how trailblazer Bonnie S. McDougall goes to China, unintentionally takes Chinese as a university subject, and develops a passion for modern Chinese literature, finally turning that into an obsession with translating it. It contains details about encounters with some of the most avant-garde writers in China in the early 1980s, followed by a different kind of fascination with the love life and sexual history of Lu Xun and Xu Guangping in the 1920s and 1930s, a story up till then neglected in Lu Xun studies. The next three chapters focus on modern Hong Kong literature, bringing these stories up to the present. The penultimate chapter deals with articles on literary translation, followed by a chapter on what McDougall calls her current obsession on the theme: "we own our own words." Altogether, this book is a story about modern Chinese literary translation and modern Chinese life, in which McDougall believes she was lucky enough to be an observer and occasional player"-- Provided by publisher.

Identifiers: LCCN 2023059512 | ISBN 9781638571889 (hardcover) | ISBN 9781638572824 (paperback) ISBN 9781638572084 (pdf) | ISBN 9781638572091 (epub)

Subjects: LCSH: McDougall, Bonnie S., 1941- | Translators--China--Biography. | Chinese literature--Translations into English--History and criticism. | LCGFT: Autobiographies.

Classification: LCC P306.92.M39 A3 2024 | DDC 495.18/02092 [B]--dc23/eng/20240227
LC record available at https://lccn.loc.gov/2023059512

Table of Contents

Preface xi

Part I: Sydney 1

Chapter 1: Certain and Uncertain Steps 3

Chapter 2: He Qifang's *Paths in Dreams* 13

Part II: Cambridge, Massachusetts, and Hong Kong 25

Chapter 3: Mao Zedong in Cambridge, Massachusetts 27

Chapter 4: Commercial and Non-commercial Transactions in Hong Kong 39

Part III: Beijing and Edinburgh 45

Chapter 5: Lu Xun and Xu Guangping in Beijing and Edinburgh 47

Chapter 6: China's Foreign Languages Press 63

Chapter 7: Shadows Poetry and Fiction 87

Part IV: Oslo and Edinburgh 105

Chapter 8: Spoken and Unspoken Words 107

Chapter 9: Shadows in Exile 129

Chapter 10: The King of Fiction in Two Places 141

Chapter 11: Translation Distractions 161

Part V: Hong Kong, Ventlinge, and Sydney 169

Chapter 12: Hong Kong Daze 171

Chapter 13: Writers in Three Places 181

Chapter 14: From *Atlas* to Love Stories to *Catalog* to
          Lockdowns 187

Part VI: Afterthoughts 197

Chapter 15: Translation Transactions 199

Chapter 16: We Own Our Own Words 215

Appendix 231

Chronology of Publications by Bonnie S. McDougall 247

Bibliography 263

About the Author 267

Cambria Sinophone Translation Series 269

Preface

The first drafts of this book were written during the COVID-19 lockdown. Looking around for something to do, I started writing about how, when, where, and why I started translating Chinese poetry, fiction, drama, and film. The book that now exists is not and was never meant to be an autobiography, and the sequence of events here, chapter by chapter, is not necessarily in chronological order but rather my reflections in the way I believe would be most helpful to readers. Nevertheless, this account starts with my earliest translations and finishes with my most recent efforts. Is it all about Chinese-to-English translation? Not quite. Have I stopped translating? Not really...

I am most grateful to Cambria Press for accepting these accounts and transforming them into a book. I also owe a great deal to a great many people for their help and advice. The following have been especially helpful, and I remain deeply grateful to them: *from Australia and New Zealand*: A. R. Davis, David Goodman, Mabel Lee, Kam Louie, Agnes Syrokomla-Stefanowska, Josh Stenberg, Michael Wilding, Paul Clark, and Paola Voci; *from the US and Canada*: Eric Abrahamsen, C. D. Alison Bailey, Edward Gunn, Patrick Hanan, Roy Hofheinz, Perry Link, Harriet Mills, and Ezra Vogel; *from Sweden and Norway*: Chen Maiping, Elizabeth

Eide, Halvor Eifring, Lena Jönsson, and Torbjörn Lodén; *from the UK*: Carole Murray, Margaret Gall, Tommy McClellan, and Guido Waldman; *and from Hong Kong*: Hugh Baker, Rosalind Cha, Chan Sin-wai, Alena Chow, Dung Kai-cheung, Gilbert Fong Chee Fun, Audrey Heijns, Ann Huss, Li Defeng, Cecilia Ip, Andy Lau, Stephen C. Soong, T. L. Tsim, Lawrence Wang-chi Wong, Laurence Wong Kwok-pun (Huang Guobin), Wong Nim Yan, and Zhang Longxi. Warmest thanks, as ever, to all friends and colleagues in China.

Words can't express how much I owe to Anders Hansson and Torkel Hansson.

Translation Stories from Modern China

Part I
Sydney

Chapter 1

Certain and Uncertain Steps

Some stories take a lifetime to understand. All my life I've been obsessed with reading and writing, but it's taken me a long time to understand that the pleasure and pain I receive from translation and research are simply a more formal extension of these two obsessions. What follows is an account of how I translate (from scribbles on paper to clumsy resorting to computers), what or whom I choose to translate (or which projects I am given), what benefits I have received from publishing translations (if any), what responses (again, if any) my translations evoke, and, insofar I can understand, why I like to translate. The depiction of my sometimes desperate and unsuccessful labors should not dismay beginner translators because, for the most part, my efforts usually turned out well. You, the reader, will have your own stories; here are some of mine.

Much of the detail in this account is from memory, but the old paper files of translations in progress that still exist and the publications themselves are the main source.[1] I don't remember exactly when I began to think of myself as a translator, only that it was a late start. But I remember being a dedicated reader since I was about seven or eight years old: one of my first memories is reading in bed by flashlight until late at night. My first recollection of utter satisfaction with reading dates from perhaps a couple of years later, when I was sitting in the sun on the front veranda with Jane Austen's *Pride and Prejudice* in one hand and an ice cream in the other (it was an illustrated edition, which I still have and read).[2] Another year or two later came my conviction that I would be a writer when I grew up. I pictured my grown-up self strolling into Dymocks (then and still the largest bookshop in Sydney) and gazing at a display with my name boldly printed on a pile of books. I had no particular interest then in what kind of books they were, but I'd guess I imagined them to be mainly fiction.

(The reading by flashlight, the sisterhood of fiction and ice cream, the stack of books at Dymocks: these are no longer memories but memories of memories.)

As these fantasies took shape, like Australian critic and essayist Clive James and around the same time as him, I was suddenly pitched from a local primary school into an opportunity school where, although I did well, I was not effortlessly the best in class but needed to work at subjects, especially arithmetic, that made my brain hurt. From that school, however, it was an easy step into a selective high school, where my schoolmates were friendly and the teachers serious. Here in my first year, I discovered the delights of French, which steered me to German and Latin a year later.

There's no simple explanation for why languages appealed to me so much. No one in my family had studied or spoken a foreign language; it may be that I had felt foreign languages extended my literacy. Whatever the reason, I was hooked. And so I flourished at high school, a brief exception being when the math teacher ridiculed me in class for reading a Georgette Heyer romance under my desk. During my third year, my parents moved to the south-coast town of Wollongong, and I completed my last two years of schooling there in relative isolation from Sydney: instead of enjoying a typical teenage social life, I read and read and read, with Tolstoy's *War and Peace* taking the longest time to finish. The fact that I was able to continue French and German also compensated for my distance from Sydney.

In 1958, I came back to Sydney to enter university, propelled by a scholarship and bursary and armed with a conviction of my abilities, little idea about which subjects I wished to study, and a dreadful fear of not being able to cope with this new life. Indeed, I often found myself misunderstanding the social cues within it. My best friend then was a native speaker of French; despite this, though, he wasn't pleased when I once addressed him in French (his Eastern European parents had been refugees in southern France). This new life, too, however, would serve as a gateway to an even greater change: by the time I enrolled, I had already agreed to go to Peking University later that year, though for several months in Sydney I was barely conscious of the enormity of this fact.

In 1957 I had been selected by the Communist Party of Australia to go to China to learn Chinese so that I could act as liaison between the Chinese and the Australian parties. It must have sounded to the party leaders like a good idea at the time: the party had already held a series of successful training workshops for local party members in China, some lasting up to a year or more. My time there was not a success, however. I returned to Australia after fifteen months instead of the five years I'd signed up for, and I never joined the party. Within a short time, there was also a decisive break between the Chinese and the Australian parties, and the liaison plans fell victim to global politics.

In the late 1950s Peking University welcomed foreign students from many countries to study Chinese. I found myself speaking French with the North Vietnamese, who were very friendly (unlike their North Korean counterparts, who stayed in a formal phalanx), and German with the large East German contingent, the best dressed and most impressively civilized students. My Danish roommate brought us an invitation to attend the Germans' musical evenings, where they played recordings of classical music, but my ignorance was soon on display when I asked why the Germans were so uncivil as to read during these recitals.

Returning to Australia a year and a half later, I worked as a librarian in Wollongong for about a year and then applied to return to university in 1961. Unexpectedly my scholarship was renewed in the second year of reenrollment on the condition that I take Chinese as one of my first-year subjects. For many years, I'd thought of that decision by the scholarship authority as a mischievous move with a political undertone; now, it seems a benevolent move to classify my absence in China as a year of study abroad, allowing my scholarship to renewed. Before then, I hadn't thought about continuing with Chinese: I'd wanted to return the exciting life on campus and in downtown pubs in Sydney but had promptly brushed aside in order to go to China.

I'm not quite sure just why I signed up for the full degree program in Chinese by the end of that first year. Although my Chinese was still good enough for some of the staff not to bother teaching me, I'd lost my spoken proficiency in the year and a half that had passed since I'd left China, and the departmental conviction that learning Chinese should start with Mencius didn't help. It wasn't then a popular course: there had been many students of Chinese descent from Southeast Asia who had enrolled, but they disappeared after that first year, leaving only a single young woman from Hong Kong as company for me. By years three and four there was only me. Departmental reforms had made it compulsory for me to take two years of Japanese, a language I never mastered but turned out to be a useful asset (see chapter 3): again, I soon ended up as the only student in this class too.

Maybe this kind of isolation from ordinary undergraduate life led to a close relationship to my teachers, in particular to the head of the Oriental Studies department, A. R. Davis, a highly regarded translator of classical Chinese poetry. In my final year, Davis taught a full year's course on Tang-dynasty poet Du Fu, which was also attended by Kam Louie (who went on to a brilliant career in sinology) as well as some staff members. Du Fu was then Davis's current research and translation subject: this led to him to steer me toward a thesis on another Tang poet Du Mu, for which I at least got to choose the poems themselves. I regret that I never tried to publish the main text or the poems in translation (though this perhaps spared me the ignominy of rejection).

As an undergraduate, I was composing my clumsy translations with pen on paper: drafting, crossing out, rewriting the whole page as it became illegible, and so on over and over again. But despite the tedium of the process, I loved it. It was partly because the poems we studied were quite short, so it was no trouble to make endless amendments for each of them in turn. It was also great fun to test the English words, leafing through dictionaries and thesauruses, trusting my immediate responses and then rewriting yet again and again after a couple of days. To translate sublime poems from a distant age that had never before been rendered into English was intoxicating, and even limited success was delightful.

Here perhaps were the roots of my obsessional approach to translation: the physical writing and rewriting, searches and research. Obsession and translation are closely related, each accentuating the other. I'm sure there are some highly gifted translators who dash off finished translations with minimal effort, and I'm certainly familiar with translations that seem never to have passed the first draft stage. Nevertheless, the pleasure that writing, rewriting, translating, and retranslating gave me now led to a resolve to tackle a postgraduate program.

I spent most of my time from 1970 to around 1986 with the translation strategy I'd developed as an undergraduate: making a complete first rough draft (easier to do with poetry than with full-length fiction); going back over the Chinese text to fill in gaps and check the original meanings; putting the new draft aside for a few days or a week or two to achieve distance; returning to assess and correct the English; and finally printing this draft, checking the Chinese, and reading the translation again.

***

Dependence on my teachers continued into my postgraduate years. Davis advised me to switch to modern Chinese for a master's degree to increase my chances of later academic employment. This time he recommended that I study the poet He Qifang 何其芳 (1912–1977) and his role in the literary and academic politics of the PRC in the 1960s and 1970s. Without much hesitation, I chose instead the poems and essays of He Qifang's early years, on which his reputation still rests. It was a choice I've never regretted. Because they were his early sources of inspiration, I needed to educate myself in modern European literature, especially poetry. Then, by the completion of my degree, I was becoming aware of how little I knew of the cultural background to He Qifang's work, so that the subject of my PhD was the introduction of Western literary theories into China in the early twentieth century. (I believe I may have chosen this subject for myself, rather than it being imposed on me.)

At the back of my mind, however, was an issue barely present in my Du Mu year but now pressing: the conflict between left-wing or communist ideology on the one hand and the seductions of European romantic poetry and the new Chinese literature of the 1920s and 1930s on the other. It only occurred to me many, many years later that Davis may have recommended He Qifang's middle years precisely so I would explore this conflict.

More practically, it was certainly a relief that the master's stipend was more generous than an undergraduate scholarship, although both had to be supplemented by house sharing and part-time work as a waitress. By the late 1960s, however, I was able to afford better living conditions and my own typewriter. Even more valuable was the gradual acquisition of university office space and the ability to spend a longer working day there. Over the next two years, my second dissertation saw my literary, linguistic, and general education occupy time that used to be frittered away in downtown social life. Not quite a student and not quite staff either, I began to spend more time with Dr. Mabel Lee and Dr. Agnes Syrokomla-Stefanowska, teachers who gradually became colleagues and lifelong friends.

Certain and Uncertain Steps

My master's dissertation won me a medal in 1967, setting me on the path of an academic future that I hadn't earlier contemplated. It also gave rise to some anxiety in my parents, who'd arranged for me to start working as a union official. In any case, I still lacked any idea about my future in mind, except perhaps to return to being a librarian: fortuitously, after completing the degree, I got a job as the university's first Oriental Librarian. This was abandoned six months later for two years as a PhD student, which was then followed by a postdoctoral fellowship that allowed me to turn both dissertations into books and embark on a career as a university teacher. It seemed at the time that this is how the rest of my life would be spent. Instead, now living again in Sydney since 2010, I've accepted translation, whether in teaching, in research, or for personal commitment, as the chief occupation in my life. I owe a lot to Davis: his influence certainly led me to academic research and translations.

***

The stories in this book were inspired by a request in 2019 from a colleague in China to contribute to a database he was constructing of translations of Chinese literature into English. In composing short commentaries on my translations over fifty-odd years, I was tempted to note some of the difficulties I'd encountered with the Chinese authorities; however, I abstained, certain that they would be deleted anyway. At the start of the COVID-19 pandemic, when it became difficult to concentrate on research, I experimented with putting those initial brief remarks into a coherent narrative. In doing so, I began to discover some continuities that I'd not previously noticed, and so the chapters on the books I've translated, along with some shorter pieces, are therefore arranged in roughly chronological order, with some overlap between the chapters due to my working on some projects concurrently.

I do not claim to be any kind of expert in academic translation studies; my 2011 book *Translation Zones in Modern China*, published by Cambria Press, is basically narrative plus description with only brief ventures into theoretical matters. It was only in my early teens that I'd been interested in abstract questions, although on my first entry into university, apart from the teachers in the course, I was the only person I knew with an interest in philosophy.

When I reentered university after returning from China and for the second time enrolled in Philosophy I, this time the subject no longer exerted its former attraction. By then I'd come to regard philosophical speculation as ever more remote, especially in comparison to the immediacy of literature. Over the next few decades, I was also becoming aware that translation studies had undergone a transformation since I'd first made its acquaintance in the 1960s and that the study of the translator herself had become a respectable subject for research. Here, putting down details of one translator's development and experience, I don't pretend to have the objectivity of distance: even the casual reader will see at once the biases that remain.

Notes

1. Over the last decade or two I've written several accounts about my life as a translator. The longest and most detailed is "The personal narrative of a Chinese literary translator." I have also drawn on an unpublished talk I gave at the Shanghai Jiaotong University in 2015.
2. Jane Austen, *Pride and Prejudice*.

Chapter 2

He Qifang's *Paths in Dreams*

My almost personal relationship with He Qifang began in 1965 with my master's dissertation and the revised book version of it, *Paths in Dreams: Selected Prose and Poetry of Ho Ch'i-fang*, my first ever full-length published translation. It consists of poems and essays by He Qifang, based on the first editions of the author's seven books between 1936 and 1945, plus three introductory essays. (Later versions of these poems and essays, published in China under the title *He Qifang xuanji* [He Qifang's selected work] in 1956, underwent extensive editorial changes that I preferred not to adopt.) Like several of my translation books, the author's name appears in the title while the jacket and title page have my name as translator and editor. This arrangement was firstly an assertion that for me, then and in the future, my translation and research would be interdependent. It was also my apparent determination that the translator be identified as the overall author of the book.

He Qifang was born in Wanxian (now Wanzhou), the first commercial port on the Sichuan side of the Yangtze River Gorges. His family, then large and prosperous, was at one point obliged to seek refuge from local banditry in the surrounding mountainous region. In later years, He Qifang lamented the sad lives of his unmarried aunts in their country fortress as well as the bloody encounter of the local warlord with British warships near Wanxian in 1926. As a student of philosophy at Peking University in the early 1930s, He Qifang found his lonely existence interrupted by Japanese attacks in 1933 on north China, but after a brief few weeks in his hometown he returned to Beiping, as Beijing was then called, where he established a literary reputation for his delicate, romantic, and wistful imagination and poetic skills. His best-known work is the long poem "Yuyan" (The prophecy), thought to result from an unhappy love affair but also inspired by Paul Valéry's long poem "La Jeune Parque" (The young fate).

He Qifang's dreamlike existence did not long survive his need to earn a living (in Beiping he'd been supported by his mother's elder uncle). Teaching first in Tianjin and then in Laiyang, Shandong, he was suddenly exposed to the combined ills of local poverty and Japanese aggression. Declarations of his new awareness characterize his Laiyang poems of 1936–1937, in which he rejects his former heroes Lord Byron and Charles Baudelaire for a style that owes much to T. S. Eliot. By the time he returned to his hometown in mid-1937, he'd become aware of the social, political, and national problems facing China, abandoning his devotion to European poetry in order to engage in political battles over the role of writers and literature in the current crisis. He obtained a post to teach at a key school in Chengdu, whose students would expect to proceed to Qinghua or Beijing universities. He Qifang at that time was already a famous writer, but the school was very conservative: as the first teacher to introduce *baihua* (written vernacular Chinese) into the school curriculum, he was one of only two teachers who were known by the students as "enlighteners."[1]

Following some months of indecision, he traveled in 1938 to Yan'an, where he declared his support for the Chinese Communist Party (CCP). Following the Chinese Communist Revolution of 1949, He Qifang spent the rest of his life in Beiping, where he served as the director of the

He Qifang's *Paths in Dreams*

Institute of Literature at the Chinese Academy of Social Sciences until the Cultural Revolution, which he survived for only a few years.

***

If I owe a lot to A. R. Davis for my academic education, I owe my experience in publishing to the novelist and publisher Michael Wilding, a personal friend and drinking companion. Together with Harry Aveling, a specialist on Southeast Asia and literary translator whom sadly I've never met, Wilding had set up the series Asian and Pacific Writing at the University of Queensland Press (UQP), where *Paths in Dreams* was published in 1976.[2] I was invited to choose my own title and cover design; for the latter, I found an illustration of an old-fashioned junk at dusk along a river. Sales were at first close to two hundred copies per annum (perhaps mostly to academic libraries?), a start whose promise had petered out by the end of the decade.

The Cultural Revolution was coming to an end, and I asked the press to set up an account with a major share of the royalties to go to He Qifang, anticipating a time when it would be permissible for him to receive it. As it turned out, He Qifang died before I had any chance to meet him or even pass on the news about the publication. I have no idea how much either of us received in royalties, but they were of course modest. Still, as described later, I was able some years later to pass on a small amount in foreign currency as well as copies of the book itself to his widow.

As an absolute beginner in published translation, I only realized after the book appeared that I'd never been given any contract for it; when I then asked, the acting editor vaguely mentioned that there was nothing about a contract on file. At some point there was mention of an American edition, but no details were given, and it never happened. In correspondence with UQP in 1979, I mentioned that the reviews in academic journals had all been excellent and that the book had also been well-received in China, with at least one good review in the Chinese literary press.[3]

Apart from *Paths in Dreams*, I also wrote a couple more articles on He Qifang and, much later, translated a handful of his poetry written and published between 1957 and 1975.[4] I was most pleased when (thanks to Michael Wilding) the poem "Clouds," one of my favorites, was reprinted in *Stand*, a literary journal based in northern England specializing in poetry. (Let me make it clear, though, that I was not the unidentified translator of the belligerent poem "No, Not This Kind of 'Peace'" published in *China Reconstructs* in January 1966.)

He Qifang's poetry and prose changed dramatically during the 1930s and again from the 1940s to the end of his life. I don't recall changing my translation style to match these changes, just adapting my text to what I found. This may sound naive, but it accurately reflects my attitude toward translation.

I stayed with *Paths in Dreams* a long time: in 1955–1956, it became my master's dissertation, and over most of 1971 it developed into a rough book manuscript. Although I had no such ambition in mind at the time, it became the first in a series of translations related to my research. I wish I could now recall in detail the translation problems that occurred and the techniques I used to solve them during those three years, but I took no notes at the time and have no recollection of any special procedures I used. In any case, I'm sure I had very little sense of translation strategies: in effect, I had none. I copied what I'd done as an undergraduate, starting with making a complete first rough draft in longhand on the reverse side of scrap paper.

The next step was going back over the Chinese text with two or three dictionaries at hand to fill in the gaps and check the original meanings. In those years, my main dictionary was the 1943 edition of *Mathews' Chinese–English Dictionary*, which I'd been given to take to China. It had been passed on to me by one of the Australian communists who had himself spent several years in China and was probably the chief organizer of my own 1950s stay there. (My own copy has long since disappeared, but my husband still has a *Mathews*.) I also recall repeated reference to a huge encyclopedia of plants so that I could trace the flowers and trees mentioned in the poems; these details could be crucial to the poem's meaning, especially if they noted whether the plants were native to Sichuan or to northern China.

When these matters were settled, I would put the new draft aside for a few days or a week or two, after which I would return to check and correct the English. The final step was to make a fair copy: as an undergraduate it would be on an old typewriter belonging to the Chinese department (where I had joint use of an office room), and a few years later it would be on my own portable typewriter in my own office. This step also included checking the Chinese and rereading the whole manuscript again.

Like He Qifang, I was fascinated by European literature generally from the nineteenth and twentieth centuries (for no apparent reason that I can now identify). Having grown up in a politically dedicated family, I was not unfamiliar with the sort of self-questioning that suffused He Qifang's poetry from 1936 to around 1940 or even the convictions expressed in his poetry after 1942. Nevertheless, I was from beginning to end absorbed by his earlier poetry and poetic essays, and I regret the comparative neglect in Chinese and other literary histories of his enthusiastically cosmopolitan and yet deeply personal writing of the 1930s.

***

My first talk on He Qifang's poetry was given in Sydney in 1967; the next occasion was in 1974, during my first visit to Harvard. Another talk was at the University of Toronto in 1976, and I gave it again later that same year back at Harvard. Most of the non-Chinese people in the audience had previously known nothing about him: he was not one of the famous names such as Wen Yiduo, Xu Zhimo, or Mao Zedong. As I was to discover, however, in China his name continues to command respect and admiration.

My return to China in 1980 came just three years too late to meet He Qifang. His early death at the age of sixty-five may have prevented his knowledge of these translations, but thanks to the Foreign Languages Press (FLP; see chapter 6), I was able to meet his widow, Mou Jueming, in 1981 and to pass on the modest royalties owed to her as well as copies of the book. Later the same year, my husband and I also met his extended family still living in Wanxian, where their old residence had been restored to them. Proud of her late husband's reputation, Mou Jueming had been surprised and disappointed that his royalties were not more generous: though an esteemed writer in China, he still counts for little abroad. In 1982, Mou Jueming agreed to a long interview with me, providing fascinating details of her own early life as well as their lives together. This was followed by a long meeting with He Qifang's childhood friend, Fang Jing. By this time my spoken Chinese had improved, and we didn't need a translator.

The following paragraphs show how pleased Mou Jueming and Fang Jing were by what they naturally regarded as an indication that He Qifang's fame had extended beyond China. Unfortunately, these interviews were set aside when my time was taken up by encounters with the new young writers who had succeeded in bringing a provocative, brilliant new wave of poetry and fiction in China in the early 1980s. In hindsight, I regret I didn't bring these interviews sooner to the attention of Western readers, to supplement *Paths in Dreams*, and update He's story. It's true that the information gained from his family and friends is not in itself immediately relevant to translation issues, even in the abbreviated form that appears later. I'm including it here even so because it's another indication of the inseparable relationship between translation and research and how fragile that relationship may also be.

***

In the first interview, Mou Jueming spoke simply and clearly, and when there was anything I didn't understand she would write it down for me. She was born in 1916 in Zhejiang, but her family moved from Hangzhou to Shanghai in 1932. She'd always loved literature, though she admitted that the *Dream of the Red Chamber* was hard to follow. She joined the Chinese Communist Party in 1938 and made the long trek to Yan'an, which included a brief foray to the front line between Chinese-controlled and Japanese-occupied territory in 1939. She met He Qifang in 1940 when she entered the Lu Xun Academy of Fine Arts's literature department, which was headed by He Qifang, and they married later the same year, with Zhou Libo conducting a simple ceremony.

Conditions in Yan'an were harsh. There were no bookshops, of course, but the Lu Xun Academy had a small library, and spirits were generally high, at least in the early 1940s. Moreover, people could take a trip to Xi'an and bring back books by Leo Tolstoy, Anton Chekhov, Nikolai Gogol, and William Shakespeare. It was around this time that Zhou Yang translated *Anna Karenina* from the English. Among their friends and colleagues at that time were writers Zhou Yang, Bian Zhilin, Zang Kejia, Qian Zhongshu, Yang Jiang, Yan Wenjing, Shen Congwen, and Liu Baiyu (but not the equally prominent writer Ai Qing, who was also in Yan'an at the time). Zhou Libo was a good friend post-Yan'an. Ba Jin was still in Shanghai. Presumably contraceptives were unavailable, though I didn't ask. Mou Jueming had five children altogether but she told me that the poor diet caused one to die of dysentery.

The family moved to Beijing in 1949, where He Qifang was given a post at Peking University before moving to the literature division of the Academy of Social Sciences (then part of the Academy of Sciences), which provided housing and other necessities. They lived in a two-story building with six rooms, two of which were reserved for their books (although books were everywhere in their home), and another one for He Qifang's study; upstairs were four bedrooms. During the Cultural Revolution, the academy lost control of the building, and the people who then moved in had no connection with the academy. By 1967 the He-Mou family occupied only the ground floor, and in 1969 they were sent to the countryside. They moved back to Beijing after the Cultural Revolution, but three families still lived upstairs, and they were obliged to sell or give away almost all of their books (about sixty bookcases). Their lives were improving as their children grew up (at the time of the interview, one son had been sent with a work team to Africa), and He Qifang became the director of the literature section of the now-reorganized Chinese Academy of Social Sciences, but the strain of the past years led to his early death.

In an interview in September 1981, presumably arranged by Mou Jueming, Fang Jing, who knew He Qifang in primary school and remained a good friend for the rest of his life, said that his late friend's best school subjects were Chinese and English, followed by arithmetic, and that he had no interest in music or sport. He was closer to his mother than to his father: his mother's family, although based in the countryside, was more interested in cultural matters than his father's. Another source by a Wanxian friend states more clearly that his playmates were his mother's young brothers, but his father was always strict, scolding and sometimes beating him. Another person from his youth said that while his mother was busy with housework, her sisters and their father took the time to tell him stories (his own work mentions his aunts' sad lives).

In his early Beijing days, according to Fang Jing, He Qifang's ambition was to write a novel, but it never eventuated; he continued to write poetry all his life, but his essays (or prose poetry) came to a halt after 1949. He wrote lots of poems in junior high school but burned all of them; later, he kept copies of his work but made no attempt to publish them. His early favorites among Chinese writers were Dai Wangshu, Bing Xin, and Xu Zhimo; he also liked Feng Zhi's poetry, but his admiration for Ai Qing was limited. Of the classical poets, his choices since childhood were unsurprising: Li Shangyin, Li Bai, and Du Fu. When it came to English writers, he preferred John Keats to Percy Shelley and put Byron below Shelley, but in Beijing he lost his taste for romantic poetry and switched to symbolism, choosing writers like Stéphane Mallarmé, Valéry, Paul Verlaine, and Arthur Rimbaud. After 1937 his preferences changed drastically, in favor of more politically active and revolutionary poets;

after 1949, when reading Russian literature was more or less obligatory, he favored Alexander Pushkin and Vladimir Mayakovsky (a somewhat odd pair, perhaps made because of the availability of their work). In its early days, the Cultural Revolution left him with few choices, so he began to learn German and set about translating Heinrich Heine's poems; he also claimed that Johann Wolfgang von Goethe's *Die Leiden des jungen Werthers* was "very strong in revolutionary poetics." Fang Jing gave a moving account of He Qifang's last days: his general health had already been seriously deteriorating when he died from a sudden attack due to stomach cancer.

***

The University of Queensland's Asian and Pacific Writing series had run for ten years and twenty volumes,[5] after which *Paths in Dreams* went out of print, so I had few copies to hand over. Oddly, but perhaps typically for UQP, I received a letter from them dated October 1986 informing me that a remaining eighty-two paperback copies were pulped in March; an outfit called Academic Remainders, however, had one-hundred copies of the paperback available for AUD$1.95. I bought up most of the paperbacks and over the rest of my time in China readily found people and institutions who were willing to accept them. In 1989 I received another letter informing me that UQP had received a request for permission to reprint two poems, for which they paid AUD$48.64 of which I was to receive some unspecified share. At least I now knew that UQP had retained a copy.

***

Paths in Dreams was my second book, following *The Introduction of Western Literary Theories into Modern China, 1919–1921* in 1971. The latter received a generous welcome from Marián Gálik, who later became a good friend (he allowed me to visit him in 1975 in Bratislava when Czechoslovakia was still an outpost of the Soviet Union). The cover design of *Paths in Dreams* was another source of pride, with a nostalgic scene of sailboats on water on its dust jacket and its handsome production inside. I received it when I had only recently signed up as a research fellow at what was then called the East Asian Research Center (later renamed the Fairbank Center) at Harvard and recall showing it off to Roy Hofheinz Jr., then the Center's director, when we happened to share a ride in the elevator. I remember in those years having full confidence in my abilities in what I saw as the full slate of translation activities: selecting (or accepting) the author and whatever part of the work that suited me; drafting and redrafting the translations; and having friends and colleagues help me find publishers. I still admire He Qifang's early poems and essays, if only for how they invoke times now long past. There is also, to me, a continuing relevance in his later battles between his early inclinations and newer loyalties.

After three years teaching at Sydney, I spent the year 1975 on research at the School of Oriental and African Studies in London. Then, after a short return to Sydney, and for personal reasons, I moved to Cambridge, Massachusetts, in 1976 as a research fellow at Harvard. The intellectual stimulation of the staff and students in East Asian studies, the extraordinarily rich resources of the Harvard libraries, and the equally rich cultural opportunities in Cambridge and nearby Boston all had an enormous influence on my life: I didn't know then and had certainly not expected that throughout the rest of my life I'd be meeting again friends and colleagues from that time whom I called on for help. I remain grateful to Harvard and to Chinese studies. At Harvard, too, was the man I was soon to marry.

Notes

1. This information was provided to me by Zhao Yihe, the head of the English Section of the FLP, on October 8, 1981. Already past retirement age, he was recalled because of the shortage of qualified staff.
2. See Michael Wilding, "Adventurous Spirits."
3. I no longer have any copies of these reviews, but UQP should have them on file.
4. For details, see the chronological bibliographies at the end of this book.
5. Michael Wilding praised the titles in "Adventurous Spirits" including my "splendid anthology," 96; the series was also praised by D'Arcy Randall, self-described as its "chief paper-pusher," 115.

Part II

Cambridge, Massachusetts, and Hong Kong

CHAPTER 3

MAO ZEDONG IN CAMBRIDGE, MASSACHUSETTS

My parents, my sister, and at least two of my uncles and aunts were members of the Communist Party of Australia, and politics dominated our lives when I was growing up. My father, quitting Scotland as a young man, had decided that the party offered the only hope for working people (which we were) and became a full-time party organizer. My mother, eldest daughter of a prominent Australian unionist, for several years worked at the party bookshop in Sydney, where I used to drop in after school. There, perched in a corner, I'd pick out Russian books I barely understood, such as Nikolai Gogol's *Dead Souls*. On some days, as a junior cadre in the Party's youth section, I'd go upstairs to plunge into meetings and activities such as locally composed drama and Russian folk dancing. In 1958, at the direction of the party's Central Committee (of which my father was a member) and with the supporting evidence of my own brief career as a Young Pioneer, my studies of three foreign languages at school, and my own naivety, I boarded a plane from Sydney to Hong Kong and went on to Beijing.

My stay at Peking University, where I studied Chinese language and politics, only lasted a year and a half, but with few distractions I learned fast. At first overwhelmed by full-time language study along with classes in modern Chinese history, economics, and politics, my own experiences as well as what I was being taught in class cast doubt on what I was learning. Twenty years later, my second translation book, *Mao Zedong's "Talks at the Yan'an Conference on Literature and Art"* (hereafter referred to as *Mao Zedong's "Talks"*) appeared in print. It's dedicated to my mother, who had died two years earlier.

Still in print and one of my most widely read translations, *Mao Zedong's "Talks"* was first published in 1980. The text itself, based on the event after which it's named, "Talks at the Yan'an Conference on Literature and Art" ("Zai Yan'an wen yi zuo tan hui shang di jiang hua"; also known as Talks at the Yenan [or Yan'an] Forum on Literature and Art), forms one of Mao's most famous writings, reprinted and circulated in uncountable figures in China and the rest of the world. A slightly edited version of two speeches delivered in Yan'an in northwest China in May 1942, it was first printed in the Chinese Communist Party's newspaper in May 1943 and appeared as a separate pamphlet later the same year. In 1953 the text was revised for republication and thereafter translated into various languages across the world. The original version was available in China with only limited access until after Mao's death and was seldom cited; the differences between the two versions were even more rarely acknowledged. In effect, the original version disappeared until the 1970s. It is now regarded as a historical document of relevance only to scholars; fortunately, there are still lots of scholars around.

It started one day in November 1976. I happened to be sorting papers piled in cardboard cartons in the basement of the Harvard-Yenching Library when I noticed a slim and slightly tattered pamphlet with a familiar title but the unexpected imprint of 1943. Reading through it, I was excited by the very different sentiments Mao Zedong expressed in 1942 about the debates surrounding the CCP's control over literature, especially literature written and published in the 1930s and 1940s. After sharing this discovery with some colleagues, I gave a paper at one of Harvard's research seminars about it, introducing the concept of Mao as a literary theorist of some weight; the second step was a plan to translate this original version of Mao's "Talks at the Yan'an Conference on Literature and Art" (hereafter referred to as Mao's "Talks"), with perhaps a one-page introductory note. The main problem was that I'd just signed up to teach a full-time job in the spring term at Harvard, greatly reducing the time I'd have for translation.

Up to that point, I hadn't been aware of the immensely valuable variorum Japanese edition of the Yan'an Talks *Mō Takutō shū* (Collected writings of Mao Tse-tung), published in 1970–1972.[1] I benefited greatly from it, despite the aim of its editors not being the same as mine. Much later, I entered into correspondence with Stuart Schram in 1994 about the inclusion of my translation in his monumental collection of Mao Zedong's writing.[2] The "Yan'an Talks" was intended to appear in the final volume (volume 8), originally scheduled for publication the following year but delayed for several years; as a result of the delay, it does not appear in most library collections. Stuart and I then lost touch for five or six years but in 2012 resumed a lively transatlantic correspondence. The first issue was about including my published translation in his collection, but we agreed that there would be no direct competition to bother either of us. As the publication neared completion, Stuart also made some suggestions about the translation; for example, we exchanged views on possible translations of *pigu* 屁股, a crucial term in the 1943 Yan'an Talks, eventually agreeing on "arse."

***

One of the first people I'd consulted about publication was Michael Wilding, back in Sydney. He'd sent me a letter in July 1976 about his plan to edit a volume of critical essays on language and literature, titled *The Radical Reader*. My original proposal was to contribute a complete translation of this early version of Mao's "Talks" with a one-page introduction and a brief bibliography.[3]

Michael was immediately enthusiastic, urging me to go ahead and suggesting that the introductory note should indicate "the changes, differences, whether political, euphemistic etc and commenting on the significance of the debates" as well as commentary on Mao and a more general discussion of Chinese literary politics. I was thus encouraged to go ahead with the translation and to supply a much longer introduction and notes on the changes. In September I had to confess that the whole package (my introduction, Mao's initial address, and his conclusion, which was five times as long as the address itself) was taking much longer than I'd expected. Even more unexpected was the "astonishing lack of accurate bibliographic information," I'd written to Michael, on the various editions of Mao's works either in Chinese or English, and that a lot that had been written about various editions was not particularly accurate. Given the interest that my fellow sinologists were showing, I'd also decided to include a list of the differences between the 1943 and 1953 editions. In short, I became involved in a much longer and substantial publication than I'd earlier imagined.

Realizing that both its timing and length were unsuitable for *The Radical Reader*, Michael declared as "a great idea" a copublication between a US partner and his own publishing firm, Wild and Woolley,[4] and if that didn't work out, his Asian and Pacific series at the University of Queensland Press might be willing to copublish.

Replying on Christmas Day, I described the current, almost complete lack of interest in Mao's literary background and interests at Harvard; only his politics counted. And so I went ahead, the project itself growing ever more ambitious with its lengthy introduction and several appendices. By June 1977, I was ready to send it to Michael for his comments. He repeated his enthusiasm for seeing the book in print, for instance with a copublication between an Australian and a US publisher. Throughout the first half of 1978 I sought publishers, preferably in the US, who would be willing to share publication with Wild and Woolley, while I continued to work on the manuscript in order to send it to him before taking off in May to Hong Kong for the summer of 1978. In turn I received a nine-page letter from Michael on authors and books I should read before going ahead with publication as well as biting comments on critics such as W. K. Wimsatt, Marshall McLuhan, and Northrop Frye. There were also lively instructions on grammar, vocabulary, and so on. All were perceptive and incorporated in the final version.

Correspondence about publication continued into 1979, with publishers including Wild and Woolley by now either unable or unwilling to accept *Mao Zedong's "Talks."* By August, I was so desperate about M. E. Sharpe, which seemed keen and then not keen and then keen again, that I offered to forgo royalties, and even went so far as to suggest personally subsidizing Wild and Woolley to the tune of US$500 to publish the damn thing; Michael suggested Hong Kong might provide cheaper deals. There seemed to be a belief that because Mao Zedong was dead, there was no point in publishing English translations of his work. At least I could console myself with the thought that I had substantially improved my own manuscript over the past two years.

Still, a savior was at hand: Harriet C. Mills, a friend I'd first met at Harvard in 1974, arranged publication at the Center for Chinese Studies at the University of Michigan. Michigan has since treated this book with great respect, and I remain grateful to all the people who had helped and encouraged me over those four years. I don't recall whether I was paid any kind of fee for the translation, and I don't think there were royalties for me or for the author himself, who died in 1976 (I've never been contacted by his descendants). Certainly, thereafter, I've paid due attention to fees and royalties, but I've always had a job (or pension) and never needed to rely on translations or other publications for a living. I've no evidence but assumed this was common practice among academics at the time.

Given the neglect of this version of the text, it required a substantial amount of paratext. My epigraphs from Paul Valéry and Cao Pei (or Cao Pi, the third-century emperor and poet) were used to suggest a tone of mutual disdain between literary authors, a characteristic of Mao's "Talks" I was eager to stress. The introduction, titled "The Yan'an 'Talks' as Literary Theory," notes that despite its undoubted importance in modern Chinese literature and history, Mao's "Talks" had rarely been analyzed as literary theory and criticism. The translation of the original edition was an appropriate opportunity to draw attention to the literary significance of Mao's "Talks" rather than its political or historical importance.

Appendix 1 lists the substantive changes (i.e., changes that survive translation; for a complete list of all changes between the two editions, see *Mō Takutō shū*). Some of these changes (e.g., the punctuation and length of sentences) are minor, and many are simply more careful or exact descriptions or terminology. Of greater interest are those which appear to be due to a policy requiring a more elevated use of language or politer form of reference. For example, *pigu* (arse, bum) is replaced by *lichang* 立场 (stand, standpoint), and *siren* 死人 (dead people) is replaced by *guren* 古人 (the ancients). "Cultural army" becomes "workers in revolutionary literature and art"; "the masses' language" becomes "a great deal of the masses' language"; "workers, peasants and soldiers" becomes "workers and peasants"; "literature and art" becomes "raw materials of literature and art"; and so on. Appendices 2 and 3 list major editions of Mao's "Talks" in the original Chinese and translated into English. The cover was sober and fittingly academic in style.

Mao's "Talks" has been subject to such minute investigation and inflated discussion that it hardly needs summary. Despite this, though, too little attention has been paid to the literary theories that Mao Zedong had presumably acquired during his youth, possibly during his term as a librarian in Beijing. It does seem odd, however, that Mao was ahead not only of his Chinese contemporaries but also of his later critics in the West in his discussion of the uses of literature as written by and for different readerships. For example, Western-influenced Chinese critics and writers assumed that urban, cosmopolitan elite writers would naturally address an elite (or potentially elite) audience; Mao, on the other hand, proposed that a relative harmony between traditional elite and popular culture was more authentic. As admitted by Tsi-an Hsia, "one does not have to quarrel so much with Mao's theory as with the fact of control."[5]

Even more unexpected is Mao's early exposition of an intuitive reception theory based on his own experience and observation, which only appeared as a fully fledged theory in literary studies in Western countries in the late 1960s and early 1970s. This feature has faded in his 1953 revised version, which veers more sharply toward the brutal authoritarian judgements of its time.

Taking up the challenge of translating a highly politicized treatise on literature, I chose to start with a typically academic task: that is, I initially focused on straightforward verbal issues from an apparently distanced perspective. I gradually became aware of how the author's voice had changed over the intervening decade. The changes were not just in the contrast between the original introductory speech and the much longer summary of his remarks in which he turned on those he'd found lacking in loyalty and reality. More drastically, in 1953, Mao was no longer a rebel leader pushing fifty in a remote and barren countryside with a ragtag collection of amateur intellectuals under his military and political command: he'd become a mature statesman and the undisputed leader of one of the world's largest countries. As for me, being fiftyish years younger than Mao and not responsible for anyone's fate but my own, I felt free to sympathize with his wit, perspicacity, and self-assurance, and to relish the task of presenting a different side of his character.

He Qifang was one of Mao's "amateurs," apparently summoned to debate questions of literature and politics but still fumbling with how to write in a way suitable to the new and frightening realities of a country in wartime; he had little experience in politics but was willing to listen to those who spoke with loud confidence. Like many of his literary comrades, he was persuaded to put aside his favorite writers and instead accompany the troops roaming in the desolate and dangerous countryside. Once committed, whatever private anguish he may have felt, he stuck to the new line, only to fall with so many others in the battles of the 1960s and 1970s. It may have been just a coincidence that in 1953, around the time that Mao rewrote his "Talks," He Qifang also edited his early poetry and essays for publication; but then, he'd always been unusually sensitive to his surroundings.

***

Mao Zedong's writings on literature and culture are no longer routinely cited even in China and are viewed as irrelevant in most countries across the world. The same can be said of a handful of translations I made of the poetry and short prose that was being written in the closing years of the Cultural Revolution and immediately after. The modestly presented *Modern Chinese Literature Newsletter*, which ran from 1975 to 1981, was generously open to juniors in the game like myself, and I happily contributed articles and translations of texts ranging from the 1930s to post–Cultural Revolution China.[6] Among the translations I submitted were the 1933 essay "Waiting for Rain" ("Yu qian" 雨前) by He Qifang, which appeared in volume 3 (1977) and two poems in volume 6 (1980), "The Paperwork Chief" by Yi Heyuan 易和元 and its relatively insipid companion "The Sparkling Milky Way" by Fang Mu 方牧.[7] "The Paperwork Chief" was distinctive in several ways, chiefly because it was accompanied by an illustration by the renowned cartoonist Ding Cong, his first return after the Cultural Revolution to the country's most officious daily press.[8] Again, the author's pseudonym was absurdly pronounced the same way as the name of the Summer Palace in Beijing, suggesting perhaps that some cadres had ample leisure time at their disposal, thus belonging to a long dynastic history of do-nothing officials. Finally, it is one of the very few modern Chinese poems for which I adopted a rhyme scheme (ABAB/CDCD/EFEF). The poems still seem, to me at least, very funny. Later my translations of poems by He Jingzhi, Fang Jingyuan, and other poets in Kai-yu Hsu's 1980 massive but erratic *The Literature of the People's Republic of China,*[9] among others, were praised by Jonathan Spence. In the end, however, I found distinctly more pleasure translating poems and essays by He Qifang and his close friend Li Guangtian, as well as fiction and other writing by earlier Republican writers such as Ba Jin and Yu Dafu. By then, thanks mainly to the *Modern Chinese Literature Newsletter* and the Harvard-Yenching Library, the selection, translation, and publication of modern and contemporary Chinese poetry and short fiction were moderately easy.

***

In the years (1976–1980) I spent at Harvard, a highly political atmosphere dominated the Chinese wing of East Asian studies, as expressed in the anti-war protests about the Vietnam War, increasing interest in the Cultural Revolution in China, and the radicalization of many students and younger academics. When Harvard professor Patrick Hanan, whose research was mostly in traditional literature and culture, published his brilliant article "The Technique of Lu Hsun's Fiction" in 1974, it was as welcome as rain in a drought. Although it was sheer coincidence that I happened on Mao's pamphlet in the late 1970s, to some extent this coincidental similar focus also echoed the then prevailing atmosphere.

It may still be of interest to consider how literary theories can be understood and misunderstood in the vicissitudes of a nation under threat of survival. From today's perspective, however, the situation in China and around the world is again deeply troubling. Efforts to differentiate shades of meaning in both literary theory and political practice as a reminder of the complexity of both are still relevant to contemporary discourse. I'm pleased that I translated this work and proud of the interest that it still evokes.

Forty years after I discovered this pamphlet, I was awarded a high-level literary prize in China. Not all of what I'd translated from Chinese authors was included in the citation but prominently listed was my translation of the 1943 original publication of Mao's "Talks." Several among the other award winners had similarly written about Mao or translated his work. Although no acknowledgement was made of the date of my source text, China's elites now publicly deemed its translation respectable.

Notes

1. Mao Zedong, *Mō Takutō shū*.
2. The revised and annotated translation, with minor agreed changes in wording, appeared in Stuart Schram's *Mao's Road to Power*.
3. At that point there were already two existing translations in English of the original "Talks at the Yan'an Conference on Literature and Art," but neither was easily available.
4. Pat Woolley was the copublisher; the firm itself only lasted a few years but gained an excellent reputation in radical literary and political circles.
5. Tsi-an Hsia, "Twenty Years After the Yenan Forum," esp. 255.
6. This newsletter, at which I became one of the editors, was predecessor to the more formal journal *Modern Chinese Literature and Culture*.
7. I am now unable to find the Chinese titles for "The Paperwork Thief" and "The Sparkling Milky Way."
8. Ding Cong (1966–2009) remains modern China's most famous illustrator and cartoonist. Subject to ridicule and abuse during the Anti-Rightist Campaign of 1957, he disappeared from public life; his poem "Paperwork Chief" was his first reappearance to the public eye.
9. Hsu Kai-yu, *The Literature of the People's Republic of China*, 527–533, 669–671, 931.

CHAPTER 4

COMMERCIAL AND NON-COMMERCIAL TRANSACTIONS IN HONG KONG

I had passed through Hong Kong while returning to Sydney from London in late 1975, but I remember little of it. One small anecdote persists in my memory: staying with Kam Louie and his wife in Taipo, I happened to observe a police-training exercise in which the police acting as protesters surged in step with the music of the popular Taiwanese song "Meilan, Meilan, Wo Ai Ni" (I love you, Meilan). Was it because they did not know any protest songs, or was it that they dared not sing subversive lyrics?

During a longer visit to Hong Kong in 1978, I happened to accompany a friend calling on the Commercial Press director who would offer my first commission for a translation. Up till then, as far as I can remember, my only financial recompense from translating had been embarrassingly small royalties from *Paths in Dreams*; however, at this point, my only income was from casual part-time teaching, so even a small fee was welcome. Perhaps because someone else had suddenly let them down, I was asked at short notice to translate the title story by Ye Shaojun 葉

紹鈞 (1894–1988) for the short collection *A Posthumous Son and Other Stories*. This story was first published in 1926, a time when the social reforms advocated in the May Fourth movement had barely penetrated beyond the Chinese population outside the major cities.

The story begins with a married couple who are happy with their first child, a girl, and with the second, also a girl, but when a succession of five more girls follows, the husband starts fearing that that the "male seed had already disappeared without trace": even his newly acquired village concubine gives birth to a baby girl. To the surprise of all, the first wife soon gives birth to a boy, who sadly dies only months after his birth. About a week later, the husband's corpse is found in the nearby river. Although the husband was known to be a heavy drinker, he hadn't been seen drunk that day, so his death remains a puzzle to the villagers. His wife, suddenly declaring she was pregnant again, continues for the next three years to announce the imminent birth of her late husband's posthumous son.

The story is a typical May Fourth product, lamenting the poor level of medical knowledge current in China at the time along with the traditional preference for male children. The good cheer of the widow and her superstitious hopes strikes a heavily ironic note for the appreciation of the more literate, semi-Westernized students and intellectuals who made up its target audience. (The famous writer, Xiao Qian [1910–1999], in a memoir published in 1984, described his awkward position as a posthumous child, his father having died before his only son was born.)

The story's title briefly presented a few problems: was the noun singular or plural, definite or indefinite? As is often the case, the Chinese title *Yifuzi* 遺腹子 seemed ambiguous at first. Thanks to the plot, however, it was clear that only one "son" appeared in the couple's life, and the indefinite was preferable because this "child" never existed. It was even more specific in that the *zi* in *yifuzi* referred to a male child. Since then, I've stuck to the convention that the main noun in a title should be regarded as singular unless there is evidence otherwise, but it was usually much harder to be certain in choosing between the definite or indefinite case.

The remaining two stories in this collection are "Lu Ma" (1948) by Sima Lanhuo and "Xiao Xiao" (1929, rev. 1957) by Shen Congwen, both translated by Lewis S. Robinson. There was no collaboration between us, and I don't recall any editorial intervention. There is a brief half-page anonymous introduction, which appeared again on the back cover; I was not asked nor did I volunteer to add more, and I am glad to note footnotes were absent. All three stories are accompanied by attractive pen drawings by someone with the pseudonym "Ah Lap" (probably a member of staff) of middle-class Chinese men, women, and children clad in traditional dress and depicted in familiar household surroundings. The cover bore the names of both translators, although its design made them almost invisible; I was not consulted about the cover, nor did I imagine that there was any need to consult me.

The theme of the collection is familiar in twentieth-century Chinese fiction: the demands of traditional families are borne chiefly by women and girls. In popular literature, sex whether within or out of marriage presents clear dangers to women; sexualized love between unmarried couples is a threat to society; and individuals can be kindhearted, but family continuance is the prime objective. All in all, some readers may find the collection is simply depressing, although it may also have been intended to disturb and energize a new generation of emancipated women in post–Cultural Revolution China. The story "A Posthumous Son" was reprinted in a Columbia University Press anthology of modern Chinese literature in 1995.

It was also on this 1978 visit to Hong Kong that I was made aware of the new literary movements that were emerging after the end of the Cultural Revolution in 1976 from writers who had written underground but were now classified as "unofficial" (that is, indicating a transition between underground and publicly open writing). Under the title "Underground Literature: Two Reports from Hong Kong," I published translations of two anonymous poems, "Not in a Dream" and "My Love," whose titles accurately represent a dramatic break from the still extant repression.[1] It was not for another couple of years that this underground movement of the 1970s became the subject that occupied my full attention for many years thereafter.

It's been suggested that my commission from Hong Kong's Commercial Press persuaded my next employer to hire me; or, more likely, it could have been He Qifang's *Paths in Dreams*. I hadn't been thinking much about which would have been better for my future employment, however. Indeed, I didn't think much then about what lay ahead.

Notes

1. See McDougall, "Dissent Literature" and "Underground Literature."

Part III

Beijing and Edinburgh

CHAPTER 5

Lu Xun and Xu Guangping in Beijing and Edinburgh

Harvard had opened many doors, and I remain thankful that among other things my four years there obliged me to face open criticism (and occasional outright hostility). My visa had expired, and it was time to move on. After considering possible options in China, Taiwan, and Japan, I applied for a position as translator at the Foreign Languages Press in Beijing.[1] My initial reception seemed favorable, and to test my qualifications, I was sent a passage written by Lu Xun 鲁迅 (1881–1936), then a prominent writer and activist, to Xu Guangping 许广平 (1897–1967). Lu Xun later published their correspondence under the title, *Liang di shu* 两地书 (*Letters between Two*). Frankly, this task was beyond my abilities at that point, and I sought help before returning it. In the end, I never discovered whether its reception had been lukewarm or enthusiastic, but I was offered the position.

In 1979 I'd married fellow sinologist Anders Hansson, and our son Torkel was born in 1980. Late in 1980, we arrived in Beijng, where my first task was to produce a full, annotated translation of *Liang di shu*. This time I enjoyed the help of FLP colleagues. For reasons described later, completion and publication were delayed until 2000, when the translation finally appeared in print under the extended title *Letters between Two: Correspondence between Lu Xun and Xu Guangping*. Because I'd made a start on the translation proper while employed by the FLP, I wasn't due any additional royalty or fee for it, and it was not FLP practice to pass on to translators any information on sales. I've no idea whether the son of the long-deceased authors received royalties, but that of course is none of my business.

Letters between Two was the most difficult, complicated, and delayed assignment of all my translations. It required the most academic research, presentation framework, and linguistic preparation; it also led to my embarking on another book that was part narrative, part analysis, and part translation, and which required my utmost efforts as well as assistance from friends and colleagues. Getting involved in Lu Xun studies was then and still is no easy venture, but I have no regrets for having undertaken this translation and remain grateful to my colleagues at the Foreign Languages Press.

The correspondence between the lovers started in Beijing, then known as Peking, with Xu Guangping writing to Lu Xun, then just her teacher, in March 1925. Letters dwindled when the two began living together in 1926 and no longer needed letters to communicate. Obliged to leave the city later the same year, Lu Xun traveled with Xu Guangping to Shanghai, and the couple then parted for the next four months, with Lu Xun in Xiamen (then known as Amoy) and Xu Guangping in her native city of Guangzhou (then known as Canton). After returning to Shanghai in early 1927, they lived together, but for appearances' sake, her room was on an upper floor and Lu Xun's on a lower floor. Some of their friends thought Xu Guangping was merely a dedicated secretary to the famous writer, whereas Yu Dafu took pleasure in speculating with fellow writer Lin Yutang that there was more to their relationship.

The actual situation between the two became evident when Xu Guangping became pregnant in 1929, prompting Lu Xun to take the train to

Peking to break the news to his mother and wife, and the lovers' final correspondence dates from these two months they had spent apart. Although their correspondence in total amounts to fewer than nine months, it underwent dramatic changes: from uneasy formality between student and teacher, to the playful intimacy of lovers after 1925, and thereafter to the calm familiarity of dedicated partners and parents enjoying a public relationship until Lu Xun died in 1936. A collection of their letters, heavily edited by Lu Xun, was published under the ambiguous title *Liang di shu* alongside several other love-letter collections that had become a trend in Peking and Shanghai in the 1930s. After 1949, the couple were described on the mainland as husband and wife, and portraits of them together incorrectly depicted Lu Xun as taller and not much older than his young wife.

Translating the title of their published correspondence proved to be a challenge right at the start. The phrase *liang di shu* (two places' letters) could be translated in several different ways depending on the meaning of *di*. It seemed too complicated to find a word or phrase that could refer to the different places where they lived in 1925, 1926, and 1929. Moreover, the most straightforward translation "two places" was awkward in one instance, when it referred to the separate households when they were living in Peking (that is, before she moved into his compound); here, "places" could be taken as referring to the two parties, but this was also not particularly meaningful either. In the end, I preferred to retain some ambiguity by not translating *di* at all: just "letters between two" was simple and adequate.

Much more challenging was developing two distinct voices to represent the two writers. He was male, seventeen years older than she, her teacher, married, an established literary figure in Peking, and reserved and formal as suited both his early upbringing and his growing reputation as a forceful social critic. She was female, young, his student, still mourning her own young lover who had not long before died of cholera, far from her home in the south, and impetuous and passionate by nature. His writing style was ironic, sardonic, elliptical, constrained, and controlled; hers was emotional, playful, spontaneous, intuitive, and bold. She initiated the correspondence, and her letters included undignified mistakes and her own corrections to some of them. Experienced as an editor of literary journals as well as his own fiction and poetry, he was ruthless in correcting her grammar and vocabulary and in deleting her political effusions when it came time for them to be published in *Liang di shu*. The stylistic gap between them shrank over time, as within a few years they grew closer, quarreled about their future as a couple, and eventually settled into marital harmony. Still, however, echoes of their original differences remained.

Lu Xun's writing style is famously crabbed, a mixture of old-fashioned and new-fangled wording in both narrative and dialogue borrowed from his native Shaoxing and later Peking years. By then I'd been reading and teaching Lu Xun's fiction for several years, however, and my own academic, old-fashioned Australian English was reasonably suitable. As was common at the time, I'd absorbed the assumption that a male voice was the norm for serious writing, to be adopted as a matter of course by female academics. Just about all the writers I had translated up until I resumed the translation of *Liang di shu* in the 1990s were male, from He Qifang, Zhu Guangqian, Zhu Xiang, Yu Dafu, Ba Jin, Xiao Qian, Li Guangtian, and Mao Zedong from the 1930s and 1940s to the more recent writers Bei Dao, Chen Maiping, Chen Kaige, Qiu Xiaolong, Wang Meng, and Ah Cheng from the 1980s. It hadn't occurred to me that a man may have been a more appropriate translator for any or all these writers or that I should pay more attention to writing by women.

Because of this, I at first found Xu Guangping's voice difficult to transmit. The only women writers I had translated before 2000 were a group of post–Cultural Revolution women poets, including Shu Ting and Wang Xiaoni, and later a novella by Wang Anyi. I needed guidance. In the final years of the project, when I was living in Edinburgh and had easy access to her work, I modeled Xu Guangping's voice after Virginia Woolf's: not just female, Woolf was also highly educated, ambitious,

Lu Xun and Xu Guangping in Beijing and Edinburgh   51

rebellious, sexually active, generous, dedicated to her craft, and only a decade older than her Chinese counterpart. For the next few years, I devoted myself to reading and rereading the entire collection of her fiction, essays, and diaries; then I pursued books about Woolf and the people she wrote about. A benefit that had become available after I'd visited Sydney briefly before moving to Edinburgh was my mother's 1930 edition of *Roget's Thesaurus*, which I used mainly to check that the English vocabulary I gave to Xu Guangping echoed her voice at that time. Whether or not readers were as drawn to the 1930s as I was, I have no way of knowing, but I've never felt that my efforts were wasted. Translating letters, in some respects, is not so different than translating poetry and essays: each letter could be treated as an individual unit, each draft of it being contained within the larger unit of the book. After drafting one letter, one could zoom out to the letters that preceded and followed it. Additionally, love letters especially are only entirely understood by the writer and the beloved: as is traditional in poetry, much remains unsaid, with layers of meaning that may never be understood by others.

Despite the inherent inscrutability of love letters, I still wonder: was my translation effective? I have no knowledge at all about the reception of this translation. Except briefly in the 1980s, it was not the practice of the FLP to send books for overseas review, so none of the work I did for the FLP imprint was ever reviewed. Or perhaps it's just that I've never been informed by the FLP of any such review.

***

By the time I embarked on the full translation of *Liang di shu*, I'd developed a policy of avoiding footnotes in literary translation, although I have no recollection when or why I adopted it. To compensate for this, I devised three levels of explication to supplement the text. As in all letter compilations, the letters themselves required a lot of background information that readers would need in order to follow the letters themselves. First, before each of the three sections of their letters, a longish note is provided to explain for English-language readers, presumably unfamiliar with the intricacies of the historical and personal background to that set of letters, how and why they were written, with particular attention given to matters that remained unspoken because they would be familiar to each party. Second, brief notes introduce the people or events specifically mentioned in the letter that would follow (although perhaps these notes could have been in a different format). Finally, there are three appendices, starting with a complete list of the letters by date from each of the two parties, followed by a list of unattributed allusions (all but the first item being to traditional Chinese writing), and finally a glossary of items that occur directly or indirectly in the main text and notes. These appendices, about sixty pages in all, acknowledge the immense body of research on Lu Xun and to a lesser extent on Xu Guangping. (I understand why some people found a lot of these appendices obstructive.)

With only silence from the FLP in the years after leaving Beijing in 1985 to settling down, after four years in Oslo (1986–1989), for a longer stay in Edinburgh (1990–2005), I had a free hand in planning and creating these supplements. My aim was to provide explanations where they would be most useful to readers, saving them the trouble of shifting from one page to another farther on. Some of this information could be provided in introductory notes to each letter, but they appear chiefly in appendix 2 and appendix 3, an arrangement that seems to undermine the point of the introductory notes before each letter. I've often wondered since then if this provision of explanatory matter both before and after the main text was excessive, putting off potential readers.

Book design was routinely created by the FLP's specialist staff without any consultation with translators, although in this case I was allowed to see some of the production process. The title and the names of the letter authors and translator are displayed on an outer paper wrapper, as well as an attractive photograph of the couple with their infant son, all set against a faint reproduction of one of Xu Guangping's early letters to Lu Xun. The inside front of the wrapper has a headshot of me and a brief biography;

at the back is a blurred photo of Amoy University and a note about the book's contents. Underneath the wrapper there's a nicely designed paperback cover, which presumably most readers overlooked; this inner cover provides a supplement to the outer cover with a reproduction of a postcard from Lu Xun in Amoy to Xu Guangping in Canton.

The book's front matter begins with a selection of five photographs, starting with the first two letters between the lovers, which reveal the striking difference between their handwriting from the very beginning of their relationship. It ends with the same family portrait as on the front wrapper, taken in 1930; here, as in other photographs of the couple together, Xu Guangping is seated with Lu Xun standing behind her, following a standard practice that gives the impression that he is the taller and stronger of the two.

Letters between Two still required a framework for inserting as painlessly as possible for the reader sufficient background information for a comprehensive understanding of a difficult text. The main problem throughout, it seemed to me, was one common to all letter exchanges, whether one-sided or representing both (or all) parties: that is, letter writers for obvious reasons routinely omit information about themselves and the outside world that is familiar to the addressees. Footnotes or endnotes are a clumsy way of addressing this problem, not only because they are distracting but because they give no sense of developments relevant to but not elucidated in the correspondence itself. In this case, information known to both parties was also suppressed for political reasons (as noted in the preface).

***

At this point, somehow a lapse of fifteen years intervened. My contract with the FLP had been suspended in 1983, but I'd stayed longer in Beijing, where I continued to translate individual texts on a casual basis. At the beginning of 1986 I left Beijing for Oslo. On a visit to Beijing in April 1986 I raised again with the FLP the possibility of completing my translation with help from two members of staff whose expertise in Chinese culture and English were among the best in the FLP's English Books section. Because my draft was still lodged in the FLP's files and still had a shortfall of some twenty letters, my proposal was rejected. On a visit to Beijing in January 1987 I raised the issue again but was unable to secure an agreement. Then in April 1989, I wrote a letter to Gladys Yang, a noted British translator of Chinese literature and the wife of another distinguished literary translator Yang Xianyi, hoping she might talk to senior members of the FLP on my behalf, noting among other things how difficult I'd found the translation, that the present version was only a rough draft, and that the appointment of a named co-translator could help bring the project nearer to completion. The then head of the FLP's English Books section admitted that my manuscript was still somewhere around but that due to the pressure of their current workload they'd never got around to planning its future. Apart from Gladys's brief report, I heard nothing more from the FLP.

Before the end of May 1989, the looming crisis in Tiananmen Square and in cities and towns throughout China became overwhelming; the final surge of violence against the demonstrations in June was met with shocked horror. Around the world, the disaster brought about huge demonstrations against the regime's brutal response. PRC's then paramount leader Deng Xiaoping is said to have commented that this international outrage would be over and forgotten within a couple of years; although his prediction never came to pass fully, there was some truth in his comment.

***

Following June Fourth, Yang Xianyi disappeared for some weeks after denouncing the government's violent suppression of protests, but he returned home in July. Correspondence with Gladys Yang then picked up again and continued for about a year. I moved to Edinburgh in 1990 and lived there for sixteen years, during which I became immersed in both teaching and administration; other translation projects also occupied much of my time. It was only when I was granted sabbatical leave at the turn of the century that I found a new opportunity to finish the translation and prepare the manuscript for publication.

First, an agreement for me to go ahead with the unfinished translation was formally made by two former colleagues, now senior FLP vice directors, in 1992; it was also suggested that copublication would be welcome. I wrote back to explain that given my workload in Edinburgh, it would not be until 1995 that I would have the time to finish all the work that still needed to be done, and another formal agreement was signed by both parties to this effect in 1995. As for copublication, which I agreed would be very welcome, I suggested The Chinese University Press, but in the end, this arrangement was abandoned.

In the summer of 1995, we made a family visit to Hong Kong, and I repeated my request for the FLP to transfer the manuscript to a diskette (as they were then called). To everyone's embarrassment, it turned out that no one knew where the manuscript was; one senior member of the English Books section suggested it may have been thrown out. In the end, thanks to the effective seniority of other colleagues and to Anders going to Beijing and jolting the FLP staff into instituting a search for the manuscript, it was finally discovered in a cupboard by one of the senior editors. I was a little agitated to find that some parts were missing, including all of part 3. I suggested that the FLP make a photocopy of the manuscript, leaving me in charge of the original; the FLP decided that they would hang on to the original but would make a photocopy for Anders to take back with him. I asked again about a disk copy because the photocopy was rather poor. I reported that Hong Kong University Press was interested in copublication; nothing came of it. Nothing came of my request for a diskette either, and I wrote again in 1997 about the poor quality of the photocopy and the continued absence of the missing parts of the manuscript. No reply followed. That year I took advantage of the long midyear vacation to spend a week in a small town southwest of

Edinburgh where morning, afternoon, and evening I could focus without interruption on the remaining letters and the book as a whole, including the missing parts. Finally, I could claim that the manuscript was complete: all that was needed was final editorial input from the FLP.

On another visit to Hong Kong, I met with T. L. Tsim, head of The Chinese University Press, who was about to make a trip to Beijing, and he very kindly offered to contact the FLP on my behalf. I asked him to let them know that the previous year I had completed a full translation of the complete text and had made a provisional index and glossary, all now on disk. On his return, he reported that there should not be any more problems. Still not hearing from the FLP, however, in December that year I sent them three diskettes covering all this material, expressing my hope that someone would check the translation itself and the accompanying materials. I also noted that The Chinese University Press was interested in copublication.

No comment, however, was made by the FLP until March 1999, when a commitment was made to publish the translation by the end of that year; it took a little longer. By the time they had responded, however, The Chinese University Press lost interest in copublication, and an email from me in November 2000 urging it to be done with another publishing house remained unanswered.

In 2000, I'd taken leave from Edinburgh to spend four months in Suzhou, where I made last-minute changes to the manuscript and sent it back to Beijing. There was a problem with the index, however. The personnel in the English section of the FLP had been augmented with new junior staff, one of whom was given the task of compiling an index. It was unusably poor. I sent the index back in July 2000 with my comments on it, and subsequently prepared a corrected index during a short stay in Beijing. I learned later that there'd been some staff turnovers.

A copy of the book itself arrived in February 2001, when I was on leave in the Netherlands. I was pleased to see the thoughtful, attractive, and informative design that the design staff had added, although a little

Lu Xun and Xu Guangping in Beijing and Edinburgh 57

disappointed that the book was only in paperback. When I turned to the index, however, I was flabbergasted to find the original defective version with its massive number of errors. Correspondence with various members of staff about responsibility for this index continued into May 2001 without any useful result. In the end, I made a new index, using the clumsy and outdated method of scanning the text word by word, paragraph by paragraph, and page by page, thus providing a complete index, which (thanks to Professor Kirk A. Denton, editor of the journal *Modern Chinese Literature and Culture* [*MCLC*]) has been available online at the Modern Chinese Literature and Culture website since 2004.[2]

Reading now through this correspondence from the 1990s and up to the last-minute issues in 2000, I'm struck by the barriers to communications in those days: the references to disks or diskettes, the business of uploading long handwritten or typed manuscripts on these disks, the long passages of silence between letters and other forms of communications. Most troubling is the way I pestered senior members of a very large key organization in China simply because I had first met them as junior staff whose main duty was to help me, and I worry now about the temerity I showed. Still, given the interest in the material itself, not to mention the long time it took to be completed and the effort that went into it, it remains a matter of regret that *Letters between Two* hasn't been given much of a welcome.

***

As *Letters between Two* slowly proceeded, the FLP assigned me in late 1981 a biography of Lu Xun by Wang Shiqing, a prominent academic expert on Lu Xun's life. At this point I still had a lot to learn about translation and about modern Chinese history and literature. The book appeared in 1984 as *Lu Xun: A Biography* (I've no idea why publication took so long). On the verso page, a member of the FLP staff is named as translator, and the coeditors are named as me and a senior member of staff. More accurately, and following standard FLP procedure, a middle-ranking member of the Chinese staff produced a draft translation, I rewrote this version into standard English, this version was then edited, and my translation was then edited by a senior member of the Chinese translation staff. Wang Shiqing was very helpful in explaining passages and references in the text that I didn't understand. The senior translator who checked and corrected my translation was also a welcome source of explanation and information.

The main text of Wang Shiqing's biography consists of four chapters plus concluding remarks; there are also six photographs of Lu Xun and a substantial index. Most of the material is well known in Lu Xun studies, but it is one of the first since the 1950s to describe Lu Xun's personal life. Most notably, Wang Shiqing's biography was the first in the PRC to mention Lu Xun's marriage in 1906 to Zhu An, a young woman from his hometown in Zhejiang; still, although she outlived her husband, she is not mentioned more than once. There was still a view in the FLP at that time that she should not be mentioned at all, but after some debate this position was deemed unjustifiable. At the time of publication, the biography was a welcome addition to English-language Lu Xun studies, much appreciated and used by me as reference guide for my translation of Lu Xun's and Xu Guangping's letters. Since then, more accomplished and reliable biographies have appeared in Chinese and several other languages, and the FLP's translation of Wang Shiqing's work is no longer in print.

Toward the end of the century, a facsimile was made of the complete original correspondence between Lu Xun and Xu Guangping. This outstanding contribution to understanding the letters is largely due to their foremost expert, the eminent scholar Wang Dehou, whom I first met at the FLP in May 1981 in connection with that year's Lu Xun centenary. Wang Dehou's main research for decades had been on the letters between the two lovers: both his publications and his willingness to answer my questions were some of the most valuable assistance and inspiration I ever received from anyone in China. Thanks to his contributions and to former colleagues at the FLP, I began to put together the material that was eventually published as the book *Love-Letters and Privacy in Modern China: The Intimate Lives of Lu Xun and Xu Guangping* in 2002.

Many years later, my research on these letters in turn led to eventual inclusion in the 2015 *History of Chinese Letters and Epistolary Culture*, edited by Antje Richter. This massive volume contains my essay "Infinite Variations of Writing and Desire: Love Letters in China and Europe" along with translations of the original versions of two letters exchanged between Lu Xun and Xu Guangping when she became pregnant accidentally and Lu Xun sped off to Beijing to let his mother and wife know before the news became public. I would dearly like to have translated the original versions of all the letters exchanged between the lovers, but it's never happened. I was able to explore some of the issues by the correspondence in articles later.[3]

***

A different path led to a burst of activity centered on exploring privacy, a concept that became a new obsession for me, thanks to the lovers' correspondence. *Chinese Concepts of Privacy*, coedited with Anders Hansson, appeared in 2002. Together with a handful of articles and essays on privacy in various publications, this book was my dominant occupation during a ten-month stay at Wassenaar as the guest of the Netherlands Institute for Advanced Studies in the Humanities and Social Sciences. My translation *Letters between Two* probably also led to an invitation to translate three of Lu Xun's essays for the collection *Jottings under Lamplight* (a title that seems a little weak, given the author's belligerent personality).[4] *Jottings* was published by Harvard University Press in 2017, nearly forty years after my early, faltering steps at translating Lu Xun in the 1980s. My contributions were "My Hopes for the Critics" ("Duiyu pipingjia de xiwang" 对于批评家的希望), "On Conducting Ourselves as Fathers Today" ("Women xianzai zenyang zuo fuqin" 我们现在怎样做父亲) and "What Happens after Nora Walks Out" ("Nala zou hou zenyang" 娜拉走后怎样). It was such a pleasure to get back to Lu Xun after so many years.

I was particularly keen on retranslating the Nora essay, not just because of its fame in China but because Xu Guangping had liked it. I was also pleased at the chance to correct the standard translation of *zou hou* as "after [Nora] leaves home": "leaving home" is what children do when they grow up; walking out is what disillusioned or rebellious women do. I would agree that *zou* could reasonably be translated here simply as "leaves"; it's the "home" that creates the problem. By this time, however, let it be clear, I was well into the ranks of the translators that I had criticized as nitpicking at the beginning of my career. More thankfully, I also received valuable advice in retranslating from (among others) the Norwegian sinologist Elisabeth Eide and staff from the National Library of Norway, which in turn led to a short article on Lu Xun's venture into Nordic literature, "Lu Xun Travels around the World: From Beijing, Oslo and Sydney to Cambridge, Mass." Above all, "Nola zouhou zenyang" (What happens after Nora walks out) remains a crucial item in Lu Xun studies with respect to his own personal conflicts and his early relationship with the love of his life.

***

The translation of *Liang di shu* had first been offered to Gladys Yang, but she'd declined on the grounds of already having too many other commitments. It was a pity, and even more a pity that it wasn't undertaken jointly by Gladys Yang and Yang Xianyi. It was an honor to be given such a key work in modern Chinese literature, and I put a lot of effort into turning out a translation and commentary designed for a substantial readership from various backgrounds. It was a disappointment to find that this book was in the end given little, if any, publicity. *Liang di shu*, together with its translation and research, still seems to me indispensable not just in Lu Xun studies and as a contribution to the understanding of modern Chinese society and culture but also a moving account of an unlikely but passionate love affair that had too short a lifetime. I've never worked harder or longer on any other translation, and despite its probably unwelcome prolixity, I remain immensely proud of it.

Notes

1. Beijing at that point was still referred to as Peking in FLP publications, although the new Hanyu Pinyin system had been drawn up for internal use in China in 1958. Hanyu Pinyin was only adopted by the FLP in 1982.
2. See also "Index to *Letters between Two*, by Lu Xun and Jing Song (Xu Guangping)," compiled by Bonnie S. McDougall, *Modern Chinese Literature and Culture*, https://u.osu.edu/mclc/online-series/index/.
3. McDougall, "Lu Xun Hates China, Lu Xun Hates Lu Xun" and "Brotherly Love."
4. See also chapter 15, where I note that *Letters Between Two* is one of the translations I take the most pride in.

CHAPTER 6

CHINA'S
FOREIGN LANGUAGES PRESS

In *Translation Zones in Modern China*, I have written an account of the structure and role of the Foreign Languages Press in Beijing; this chapter details my personal relationship with the organization. I'd been familiar with the FLP, founded in 1952, since I was a child visiting my mother at her bookshop, deepening this familiarity later while exploring a backroom used as a bookshop in my father's party rooms in Wollongong. Skip to 1978 when I was at Harvard and trying to find a publisher for my *Mao Zedong's "Talks"*: a friend then living in China suggested that I consider translating for the FLP. I'd become keen on the idea of living in China again, this time as an adult and not a teenager, but didn't yet see the FLP as a potential employer.

The thought of working at the FLP rather than remaining a casual contributor popped up again around a year later, when it was becoming clear that choices about where to live were becoming limited. We'd also considered Hong Kong or Japan, but in June 1979 I applied directly to the FLP for a job, sending my translations of two recent poems by He Qifang.[1] There was no response. I then wrote to the Foreign Experts

Bureau in October, asking for a job at either the FLP or the Chinese Academy of Social Sciences. Again, no response.

In November I wrote directly to Yang Xianyi and Gladys Yang. My letter begins with my proposal to arrange for the late He Qifang's family to receive the author's royalties (which I warned were modest) and ends with my request for a position at the FLP. In December I received a reply from Yang Xianyi and then one from Gladys Yang. Both were warm and friendly, offering hope that a position would be available.

In February 1980, Gladys Yang sent me a "strictly unofficial" letter about translating *Liang di shu*. She had declined to translate it herself, being fully committed to other projects, and so had passed on my name to the English Books section at the FLP; at the same time, she warned me that it would not be an easy task. This I was soon to confirm.

Next came a letter in March 1980 with an offer from the head of the English office of the English Books section for a two-year position as a "polisher," along with an immediate task as a test, the translation of Lu Xun's preface to *Liang di shu*: "[It] will need to be completed within ten months so that it may be published next year, in time for the centennial anniversary of Lu Xun's birthday." I replied explaining that for personal reasons (my first child was due in April) I couldn't move to Beijing until later in the year; in the meantime, however, I would surely be able to return a complete translation of *Liang di shu* by September.

Some confusion followed when the Foreign Experts Bureau wrote offering me a position as teacher, which I politely declined. Then another senior member of the English office sent me a sample extract from *Liang di shu* in April, explaining again the urgency of the translation and the difficulty of the text. It was much more difficult than the Chinese materials I was accustomed to reading, and I begged for help from my Harvard friends. It was graciously given, and I submitted the translation at the end of May. In the meantime, I received and returned rather desperate letters about when I should return the sample paragraphs, complete the whole book, and receive a definite offer of employment. Our son arrived on April 30, and my attempt at the Lu Xun sample was returned on May 30; the FLP and I continued to swap information about how I might be employed and when we should come to Beijing. On October 1, my husband, son, and I left Boston, and after a short stay in Stockholm arrived in Beijing on October 8. The three years I then worked full-time at the FLP upgraded me from an amateur translator to a professional.

***

In Beijing, we were provided with accommodation at the Friendship Hotel (*Youyi binguan*), the designated accommodation built in 1954 for "foreign experts" (that is, non-Chinese people working for various branches of the government or party). There were some drawbacks in this closed community, and the term "loony binguan" was in common use. Like most of the other inhabitants, we chafed at the pervasive presence of armed guards and the rudeness of hotel staff to Chinese visitors. I explained in a letter to a friend that in some ways it was like living in Cambridge: there were lots of Americans around, and our apartment was small, with high ceilings and lots of cockroaches.

Our workday was long: 8:00 a.m. to 5:30 p.m. five days a week, with an additional half day on Saturday, and we were bussed to the FLP some twenty minutes away. Neither our living quarters nor the office I shared with five other people could be described as comfortable or agreeable, but that wasn't a problem in the first few months. Instead, I relished the opportunity to act as a kind of liaison between the Chinese literary and translation world and sinologists in English-speaking countries: for instance, I reported and wrote for the Harvard-based *Modern Chinese Literature Newsletter*, forerunner of *Modern Chinese Literature and Culture*. The transformation a few years later of the *Newsletter*, of which I was one of a group of editors, into a full-scale academic journal led to a call for the *Newsletter* editors to resign; I chose to be difficult, refusing to resign, at the same time making it clear that I would accept the decision to be dismissed without demur. I had yet to learn how to win friends and influence people.

My initial salary in Beijing was five hundred yuan a month; it was increased after my probation to seven hundred yuan. As foreign experts (as we were known; "foreign friends" was the term for a lower category of employees such as students) we enjoyed a special allowance for a one-month annual vacation plus reduced rates for travel and accommodation. Housing at the Friendship Hotel was free, as well as medical expenses except for a small service charge. In addition to our monthly salary, the cost of travel (including a luggage allowance) to China and back home was paid for two-year recruits (one-way for one-year appointments).

A problem occurred when I asked for contraceptive pills at the FLP's on-site medical center: they referred me to the FLP's senior Party member. Accompanied by an office colleague, I was taken back when the senior Party member, a middle-aged man, opened a drawer, shuffled some papers around, and pulled out a bunch of pills. I never went back.

At the Friendship Hotel, we employed for our infant son a full-time baby minder, a middle-aged woman with lots of experience and a great deal of kindness. At special events like New Year celebrations at the office and on excursions to local scenic sites, our son usually came along and was given loving attention by our colleagues; one officious member of staff, however, once chastised one of the new junior translators for paying him too much attention.

Expeditions during working hours of various kinds were frequent, some involving the whole office, others arranged for experts only: the main problem with the latter was that we were rarely told until we reached our destination where it was that we were going or for what event. The best account of our somewhat depressing working lives is the essay "My Days in China" by Rashid Butt, another foreign expert, in the compilation *Living in China*, published in 1979 by the New World Press (another unit within the FLP).

At first all seemed very rosy. My workload in the FLP's English Books section was heavy but mostly of interest, especially when I had time to work on *Liang di shu*. My work also included tasks for other units within the FLP; in January 1980, for example, I processed an article on linguistics in *Beijing Review*. I also enjoyed the company of my office colleagues: one older woman took a kind interest in my health and showed me a form of yoga-like exercises, designed for women who'd just given birth, to practice at our compulsory mid-morning breaks (not everyone used these breaks for exercise). Some colleagues took their work lightly, reading newspapers for an hour or so before attending to work; others, especially the juniors, were very conscientious.

I was also very conscientious in the beginning. Although I wrote to colleagues outside China that I was very happy working in the FLP's English Books section, the long hours still affected my health, and I was often ill, typically spending the weekend in bed feeling wretched, recovering by Monday to return to work, only to fall ill again the following Saturday. My colleagues at the FLP were concerned and pressed on me a heavy dose of vitamins A, B, B1, C, and D, together with yeast and calcium (which brought me some relief). Looking around me, I also decided that I should probably copy my coworkers and try to take it easy. It wasn't hard to do, and there were plenty of distractions at hand. Still, I remained in poor health throughout the winter of 1981 and well into spring the following year.

It was apparent that in late 1981 and early 1982 that the situation for Chinese intellectuals had become tense. In a March 1982 letter to a colleague in the US, I remarked (referring to a rising young poet whose work I admired and had translated) that "a young man should not draw too much attention to himself with foreign mail." The tension eased a little the same year, only to return in a more virulent form in 1983. Again, resistance turned out to be effective, and in the years 1984–1985 the intellectual and cultural world began to flourish in a way no one could recall: it was like the May Fourth movement all over again.

***

After I met Mou Jueming (see chapter 2), I continued to be invited to meet members of the Chinese literary elite who held a high opinion of He Qifang (my *Paths in Dreams* had some circulation in China, though I hadn't realized it then). The FLP arranged a meeting in January 1981 with the distinguished elderly writer Zhu Guangqian at his home at Peking University (I had written a long article on him while living in London in 1975). Zhu Guangqian was then in his early eighties, but happily for us he was still fond of a glass or two of some alcoholic drink in the morning. We found out only later that he'd been informed that I was the New Zealand writer Katherine Mansfield (1888–1923) and that my husband, Anders, was the English literary intellectual John Middleton Murry (1889–1957).

Soon after, Zhu Guangqian was a front-row guest at the January 1981 Burns Night, organized by a Scottish colleague at the FLP, at which I recited one of the longer poems from *Paths in Dreams*. Zhu, who'd spent some years at Glasgow University in his youth, particularly enjoyed the miniature bottles of Scotch that were presented to the front-row audience. In May, Zhu made a return visit to us for afternoon tea at the Friendship Hotel, bringing with him the last postgraduate student of his long academic career, Zhang Longxi. Zhu Guangqian died in March 1986. Although I was no longer employed by the FLP, I was grateful to be commissioned to translate for *Chinese Literature* one of his essays, "A Comparison of Chinese and Western Poetry," as a tribute.

Such events added much to our stay in China, although we came to feel less comfortable as the general atmosphere became oppressive. In March 1981, my female colleagues and I, mainly foreign experts, were dismayed by the organization of International Women's Day. It also became noticeable that within our section and presumably throughout the FLP, staff were deeply split as new ideas and old beliefs contested the new realities. It soon became obvious, for instance, that some of the senior members of the translation staff at the FLP were deeply cynical about the nature of the works selected for their attention, whereas for the middle-aged and junior staff their translation duties constituted little more than a boring office job in an environment that was not particularly convenient or interesting.

I had little contact with senior administrative or editorial staff, but the main duty of the FLP was clear: to transmit approved knowledge of China to the rest of the world. What was evidently under acute debate during the 1980s, even reaching the low-level offices of the translation staff, were questions of just what kind of books, journals, and other publications were to be published.

By 1981, I'd become viewed by my English Books section coworkers as a useful colleague and consequently problems, both professional and domestic experienced by or with foreigners, were often placed on my desk. I was quite willing to take care of these matters, and they certainly increased my understanding of office life in Beijing. The most harrowing commission was the case of a European woman who was having difficulties with personal problems and had resorted to alcohol; within a few months of her arrival, she'd become almost a hermit, only venturing from her room to buy more liquor from the local stores. The next steps involved Chinese and foreign doctors as well as senior levels within the FLP and her own embassy. Eventually, agreement was reached that she should be repatriated, but on her return journey she disappeared during a stopover in Europe. At that point, it was no longer a problem for the FLP: her relatives stepped in, located her at the airport, and brought her long journey to an end. It was a sad and difficult time for everyone involved.

***

Often enough I charged headlong into offering advice on various matters without having been asked to do so. Gladys Yang at one point advised me not to be so pushy, but I persisted. One initiative soon after our arrival was drawing up a schedule to distribute to fellow foreign experts showing the opening times and addresses of the clusters of shops at the Friendship Hotel (at the time, each shop had its own hours, and it wasn't anyone's job to address or publicize them). An attempt in December 1981 to rationalize contributions led to drafting rules for presenting translation manuscripts to the FLP for consideration: for example, "the manuscript must be typed in triple space, with right-hand margins of at least 1.5 inches...It is particularly important that notes and quotations be typed in triple space as well" and so on and so forth. Someone should do it, so why not me? But not everyone thought it was any of my business.

For reasons I no longer understand, in December 1981 I also drew up a two-page document explaining why the section on literature in a new FLP handbook was deficient. (Was I asked, or did I volunteer? I have no idea. Was it effective in introducing change? No.) My enthusiasm for correcting others also extended to *Social Sciences in China*, the journal of the Chinese Academy of Social Sciences, for which I was asked in June 1981 to evaluate an article on Wang Anshi, a famous Song-dynasty politician and poet whose work I barely knew. By then I'd already embarked on a one-woman feminist crusade that continued throughout my employment. In December 1982, for instance, I was asked by the magazine *Women of China* to comment on a recent issue of their journal: I responded with a highly critical screed that the editors promptly filed away.

One encouraging move became standard in 1981–1982: sending the younger translation staff one by one to study at US universities or colleges, such as Amherst College. The letters I received from them when they were in the US showed an impressively high level of English proficiency, and to that extent the scheme succeeded. Less impressive was the staff's understanding of cultural differences. On one hand, an account of Christmas was beautifully described by one mid-ranking translator; on the other hand, her main recommendation on returning to Beijing was that the Friendship Hotel rooms should be equipped with chandeliers (and so they duly were; they were quite modest items, thankfully, not the massive chandeliers of formal buildings). A member of staff, who had been sent to the US to improve her English and understanding of Western society, turned up on her first day back wearing a bright red jumper; by noon, she felt obliged to take it off because of the unpleasant comments and sidelong looks she was getting. Even after the end of the Cultural Revolution years, for a married woman to wear colorful clothing was regarded as disgraceful. To make matters worse, she explained, her single offspring (in line with current policy) was a boy and wouldn't be willing to wear a red jumper.

The most serious episode I was involved in concerned the Friendship Hotel staff's weak safety measures, which resulted in a crisis in May 1983. Foreign residents had made repeated complaints about access to the balconies around the main southwest dining room, which were used by staff for storing mops and other equipment and for ventilation. In principle—but not in reality—the doors to the balconies were supposed to be kept locked, and the lackluster responses by staff to repeated complaints made by the foreign experts about safety were perfunctory at best. With easy access to the balcony, a small child wandered out one day, fell over the low railing, and died.

***

As a full-time employee in the FLP's English Books section, I was on occasion drafted to translate for the Chinese Literature section, which usually came as a relief from the routine duties I was then being allocated. The Chinese Literature section was initially established as an independent unit in the early 1950s to publish the magazine of the same name but soon became a section within the rapidly expanding new FLP. My tasks there were mostly welcome. Most notably, they included Wang Meng's splendid "Voices of Spring" ("Chun zhi sheng" 春之声) and a selection of poems by seven women writers: Zheng Min, Wang Erbei, Zheng Lin, Lin Zi, Shu Ting, Bai Hong, and Wang Xiaoni; the choice of which writers and poems was probably made by senior members of the Chinese staff under the tactful influence of Gladys Yang. As far as I now recall, I translated directly from the Chinese on these occasions, and although my draft was overseen by a senior member of staff, I received sole credit.

One of the most successful initiatives at the Chinese Literature section in the 1980s was the appearance of the Panda Books series, founded in 1984. This new series was designed as a conduit for paperbacks meant to reach a broader audience than that of the English Books section's often excessively long and weighty hardcover books, whose authors were (or had been) loyal party supporters. Yang Xianyi, who by this time had reached a senior level within the FLP, was among those planning to showcase the newly relaxed guidelines for publishing books for foreign readers. Gladys Yang was the most notable of the full-time translators to be seconded to Panda Books, but other members of the FLP and outside personnel, including suitably qualified foreign staff, were also recruited. The result was a sudden flurry of books designed for a broader foreign readership than had previously been the case at the FLP.

***

In one instance, I was gratified by being given an editorial role. It was probably then that I first met Xiao Qian, and we soon became good friends and colleagues. (Many years later, I realized that he had been among those who knew of *Paths in Dreams*, forming yet another link for me with the Chinese literary world.) Xiao Qian's book *Chestnuts and Other Stories*, published in 1984, begins with a brief description of the author's life and publications in English and Chinese, highlighting his impoverished childhood, early literary career, and adventurous life abroad in wartime Europe. The title page notes that the translations are by "Xiao Qian and others"; it is followed by my preface, which gives a little more detail. "Chestnuts" ("Lizi" 栗子) was originally the title story of the author's second collection of fiction.

Chestnuts and Other Stories has almost all the same contents as Xiao Qian's *The Spinners of Silk*, published in London in 1944 by George Allen and Unwin; four of the latter's twelve stories first appeared in English-language journals (including *The New Statesman*) and an anthology. In his acknowledgements to this edition, the author thanks English friends and colleagues for their "criticism and corrections"; although not explicitly mentioned, it would have been understood that the author himself was also the translator.

Eight of the original twelve stories in *The Spinners of Silk* were reprinted in *Chestnuts*, along with a 1980 memoir and three more stories dating from the same period. One was translated by Elisabeth Eide, another by Xiong Zhenru, a member of the Chinese Literature section, and the third by me, although our respective contributions are not identified. In the preface I noted that the author's often free translations or adaptations had not been altered for the Panda edition except for minor changes in spelling and notes.

One of the stories from *Spinners of Silk* that was omitted from *Chestnuts* was its title story, a romantic account of a teacher and his girlfriend raising silkworms; the others omitted are short and not of any special interest. The most notable addition to the Panda edition is the author's memoir, "An Album of Faded Photographs," which is an autobiography detailing his impoverished childhood and youth. Most of the stories in *Chestnuts and Other Stories* portray the wretched existence of the poor and unprotected in early twentieth-century China; others depict his own remarkable passage through school to a highly successful career as a journalist, editor, translator, and fiction writer.

Except for this memoir, the other works in *Chestnuts and Other Stories* were all written between 1933 and 1937, when Xiao Qian was living in Peking. He left for England in 1939, and after a prolonged stay abroad that included a spell as a war correspondent in Europe, he returned to China in 1946. Xiao Qian was one of the first Chinese writers to portray in fiction the sometimes disastrous effect of the Christian missions on individuals, especially children and young men, in China. His story "The Conversion" on this subject was included in Edgar Snow's 1936 anthology *Living China*; it attracted more attention from contemporary reviewers than any other story in it and thereafter became a standard anthology item.

In his introduction to *Living China*, Snow thanked (among others) Xiao Qian, described as the editor of the *Ta Kung Pao Literary Supplement* who introduced Shen Congwen and Ba Jin to Snow and who translated some of the stories in *Living China*. Nym Wales (the pen name of Helen Foster Snow, Edgar's wife), who contributed an appendix on the modern Chinese literary movement for the collection, describes Xiao Qian as a follower of Shen Congwen's "independent Romanticism." It appears, however, that the Snows were not in direct contact with Xiao Qian.

Some of Xiao Qian's early stories in *Chestnuts* are affectionate evocations of traditional Chinese folk arts and festivals, perhaps based on his early childhood before he became fully aware of his background. His father, a member of the Mongolian imperial guard, died shortly before his son was born, but his Han mother remained dependent on his father's family. Xiao Qian recalled the ignominy of being derided as a posthumous son, and it was only in the 1980s, when new protection was offered to ethnic minorities, that he took pride in his Mongolian background, which for many years he had hidden.

In the wake of Japanese encroachment and outright invasion of China in the 1930s, many writers, along with large swathes of the general urban population, moved to the interior. Some, however, stayed in Beijing or Shanghai even under Japanese rule: Xiao Qian was one example, although he lived in China only briefly during that time. His stories included accounts of his impoverished family, his early education in work-study missionary schools, and the harsh working conditions he experienced after leaving school. Xiao Qian later wrote that he deliberately practiced a form of self-censorship by making most of his characters children; in this way the author conveyed indirectly his resentment toward all foreigners in China, not just British missionaries and Japanese invaders, as well as the Chinese whose main interest was to placate these foreigners. "When Your Eaves Are Low" describes the poverty to which the author was exposed in his childhood, and "The Philatelist" shows his awakening to the harsh reality of Japanese aggression in north China. "Galloping Legs," about the tragic fate of a rickshaw puller, was praised by the *Times Literary Supplement* in 1944 as "almost the best" in the original edition.

Many of his native readers in the 1930s would have been aware of the deeper level of meaning in the stories about children and young people, but they escaped the attention of the authorities. Through his choice to speak through naive voices, Xiao Qian achieves a delicate balance between sympathy for his protagonists and condemnation of the oppressive society in which he grew up. Xiao Qian's career as a fiction writer was limited, however: he left China for the UK in 1938 and thereafter lost the impetus to write fiction.

***

As well as occasional work for the Chinese Literature section, which was never a burden, I was also given assignments for the Beijing Review section, which, like the Chinese Literature section, was in the same building as the English Books section. Not all of these items are included in my online curriculum vitae: one instance was an early article by Mao Zedong in which he favorably mentions Hu Feng,[2] and for that reason had not been included in Mao's 1953 collected works.

One of my more interesting assignments in the English Books section was an up-to-date guidebook to Beijing to cope with the increasing number of foreign visitors and tourists coming to China. The usual stiff language of official data instead of information for individual first-time travelers to China was evidence of the editors' lack of any contact with foreigners, and eventually I was allowed (with help from Anders) to visit the places mentioned and provide details that would be welcomed by visitors with little or no previous knowledge about traditional or modern China. It was just at this time that renovations were made to religious sites, including ancient temples and courtyards of various kinds. Of course, such a handbook had a limited shelf life and rapidly became out-of-date, but for the time being it provided updates to elderly copies of Nagel's thick guidebook for China from the 1960s[3] and other guides. An example of the sensitivity that arose even in humble guidebooks for tourists was the description of a high-end gourmet restaurant at the Summer Palace, which required the diners to pick up live shrimp with their chopsticks and dip them in boiling liquid before consuming them. My suggestion to delete this item in the text was accepted, but Anders criticized me for acting as censor.[4]

One useful skill I picked up at the FLP was to increase my awareness of the parallel systems of punctuation in operation in the UK and US. A more sophisticated technique I also learned was the principle of compensation, where an expression or concept that is not easily translatable at first encounter can more easily be slotted in at a later stage of the text. Even more to the point was the hard slog of constant reference to all kinds of dictionaries and reference works and endless persistence in continual revision. Working alongside talented junior and senior staff left me with a lasting conviction of the huge advantages of teamwork for the different personalities. For example, Gladys Yang was typically blunt, would not hesitate to rebuke me for my failings in professional or personal conduct, whereas Yang Xianyi was infinitely tolerant.

On the whole, and despite my ignominious dismissal later on, my previous account would seem to indicate that translation and translators were well treated and highly regarded in the PRC. I am not sure, nevertheless, that this was really the case. The main disadvantage of working for the FLP in the early 1980s was its rigid system of rules and restrictions. One example was to add words like "Province" or "City," always with an initial capital letter, after every place name, presumably because of an edict that all information conveyed in the original text must be transferred to the translated text. More troubling was that the quality of the material to be translated was often mediocre at best. For example, although the translators were essential to the organization, it seemed to me that with the exception of some of the senior translation staff, the translation sections were at the bottom of the organizational ladder: the editors had more power to determine what should be translated, even if they knew no foreign language or had no experience of living abroad. The authoritarian structure of the press also meant insensitive supervision of our working and private lives. In this, the FLP then was in many ways a truly awful employer.

***

Of all the sections at the FLP, Chinese Literature was probably the most relaxed and adventurous, thanks primarily to the Yangs and the staff they recruited. Qiang Geng's 2020 article "Gift-giving: Panda Books Series and Chinese literature 'walking toward the world'" suggests that with this section, the FLP was offering a gift to the world. The concept is attractive, but the difficulty here is conflation of a gift (an item that is free of charge to the recipient from a person, or commercial or institutional body, to another) with an item designed to be purchased.[5] Because the books published in the Panda Books series are sold to readers, they do not qualify as gifts. In a very general sense, it can be claimed that every book ever published is a gift to readers, but it is doubtful if the notion of gifts can be extended to products that are sold to them.

Qiang does not attempt to assess the reception of works in the Panda Books series in the countries to which they are sent. Maybe this is not important in his study, which is focused on the intention of the publishers and only to a lesser extent of the translators. Nevertheless, it was clear enough to the Panda translators that their books were poorly marketed abroad. They were rarely reviewed in the American, British, or Australian press and rarely appeared on the shelves of big commercial bookshops. In the 1950s and 1960s, FLP products had for the most part been only available in left-wing bookshops or Communist Party rooms. After the end of the Cultural Revolution, when Panda Books began to appear in bookshops with a particular interest in China, their reach became only a little wider.

A question that is not resolved in Qiang's article is whether or not a translation gift is one that is made by a translator, either alone or with colleagues, or by a commercial or political unit. In practice, it is not common to describe a publisher (or even a nation state) as making a gift of a translation to an unknown readership, especially when the material has nationalistic or political purposes. If this process were to end with a gift, it might be expected that the translator is an individual who undertakes a translation without expecting a financial or other kind of reward. On the other hand, when a person (or team) is assigned a work to translate by a publisher who provides them not only with a salary but also their housing, medical needs, and more, the transaction can hardly be described as a gift from the translator to the reader. Even more unlikely to qualify as a gift would be the publication of a literary translation by a state-funded company for an unknown readership.

It should be acknowledged that even in the context of a large and well-funded organization producing translations for an overseas and unknown readership, a translation can still be regarded as a kind of gift from the translator herself. Gladys Yang (who is only briefly mentioned in Qiang's article) was a personal friend of Chinese women writers as well as self-appointed translator of their work. In particular, she was dedicated to the cause of women who, like herself, had suffered devastating experiences, including years in solitary confinement in prison during the Cultural Revolution. Even though other senior translators also had personal or professional links with well-known writers, such direct involvement in the process of selection and translation was not common in the FLP, perhaps infusing the translations process in the FLP with gift-giving more than one may think.

***

I was introduced to the poet Qiu Xiaolong at the 1981 Burns Night; at the time, he was a postgraduate student at Peking University, supervised by Bian Zhilin. In addition to translating his own poems into English, he had translated T. S. Eliot's works into Chinese. I was impressed by his fluent, if erratic, English, knowledge of modern English literature, and commitment to contemporary Chinese poetry. Of all the young writers I met in China in the 1980s, he was the only one whose knowledge was good enough for co-translations.

In early 1981, we agreed to co-translate some of his poems, with each of us making separate drafts and then meeting to compare them, sometimes achieving quite different results. By this time, he'd returned to Shanghai, where he'd obtained a junior post at the Shanghai Academy of Social Sciences. Now that our face-to-face encounters were few, each of us was to produce a draft translation and then exchange opinions by letter; oddly enough, this arrangement seemed to work. The first of our collaborations appeared in the Western Australian journal *Westerly* in 1981, alongside more conventional efforts by the Cultural Revolution survivor Feng Jingyuan as well as a poem by Zou Difan, a prominent figure in the poetry establishment of the early 1960s and late 1970s. (I particularly liked Zou Difan's "Sunflowers Bright He Selected," an appealing 1961 short ballad about a man who gives his sweetheart sunflowers instead of roses.) According to a letter from *Westerly*'s editor in April 1982, the China issue had "attracted a good deal of favorable comment."

A further selection of five poems by Qiu Xiaolong, also co-translated, appeared in the 1983 anthology *Stubborn Weeds*, edited by Perry Link.[6] The poem "Street Scene" has a strong element of post-Eliot influence, which, according to the author, was popular among his fellow poets; another poem "Lost Identity" was one that Bian Zhilin particularly liked. None of these poems were rhymed in the original but while we were translating "Lost Identity," the rhyme first appeared spontaneously, and with a little extra effort and the author's agreement it was worked into a regular pattern. I also argued the case for substituting a word or phrase with a different literal meaning with a class resemblance to the original, such as translating the word for "leaf" as "grass," both falling into the category of small green plant life.

Qiu Xiaolong's subsequent status became compromised after a disastrous encounter with a visiting British academic, who'd punched a policeman and then disappeared from view for a week or so. While this man was hiding from police, Qiu Xiaolong inadvisably tried to retrieve some manuscripts he'd left with him and was promptly collared for his association with him. Although I was not personally involved, Qiu Xiaolong avoided meeting me again in China; many years later, I noted with interest that a rather unpleasant and ignorant woman called Bonnie appeared in one of his crime novels written after he moved to the US. We finally met again in Sydney at a well-attended University of New South Wales Confucius Institute event, all rancor long buried.

Qiu Xiaolong and Zou Difan were both among the large circle of writers young and old, famous and barely known, who turned up regularly for an evening at the Yangs' small flat in the residential buildings at the back of the FLP. In this relaxed (and occasionally drunken) group, it was encouraging to find people openly expressing their opinions and expectations. Perhaps some of these visits were self-serving: foreigners and Chinese looked for each other because of their usefulness to one another. Still, regardless of anyone's opportunistic motivations, the Yangs undoubtedly created an environment where all of us could feel at home. I was about to stray from this comfort into a more challenging environment, however.

In the meantime, on a personal level, an embarrassing episode occurred far from our home base: Anders and I were traveling to Shanghai and Xiamen in the company of a senior member of the English Books section staff, with the purpose of visiting the place where Lu Xun had written letters to Xu Guangping. In Xiamen, we also had arranged a meeting with Shu Ting, who lived in Gulangyu and had invited us over. I'd translated some of her poems for *Chinese Literature*, and the visit seemed to go quite well. Just before we left, Shu Ting drew me aside and told me that the senior translator who accompanied us had warned her that I was extremely mean. It was true: I never became accustomed to the Chinese law of hospitality that decreed masses of food should be left over at any meal shared with guests, and often found myself clearing my plate. Despite both parties feeling aggrieved, we continued our journey and sat at one table for meals; after all, we were both paid employees of the same firm.

***

Toward the end of my employment, I was assigned to translate plays from the 1930s by Guo Moruo 郭沫若 (1892–1978), a prominent writer of his time as well as a left-wing scholar and activist, some with me as the sole translator and some with a co-translator. These translations were published as part of *Selected Works of Guo Moruo: Five Historical Plays*. Feng Fumin and I had translated four of the plays, with the Yangs translating the remaining one. Guo Moruo was as far as I was concerned one of the less attractive of the May Fourth writers, but as a matter of course I took on the assignment. It so happened that one of the plays was being performed in a Beijing theater, and I was dispatched there in the company of an academic specialist who was on occasion recruited by the FLP for advice. The theater was half empty; not long after the curtain rose my companion fell asleep, and I wished to do so as well. Like much of the work I did for the FLP, I've not bothered to list my Guo Moruo translations in my CV.

Despite these discomforts, it was still an exciting time to be in China, for foreigners as well as locals. With a few exceptions, I'd been well treated by the FLP's high-level managers, editors, and translators. Many of my assignments were agreeable, although not all required much thought. Still, some offered opportunities for our imagination, such as translating elaborate recipes with fanciful names to be served at the Great Hall of the People, the grand meeting place where Chinese legislators convened and visiting heads of state and government were entertained. I was also asked to work on Ai Qing's poetry, which was not much fun; of more interest was a lengthy new history of China by a Bai-nationality scholar. As I worked through many of these projects, though, I was bothered by repeated deferrals of *Letters between Two*. Certainly, the generous hospitality we enjoyed at the Yangs' residence and stimulating meetings with Chinese writers, critics, and academics helped us retain our sanity. There was also good company among the FLP's foreign experts in other sections, including Chinese Literature, Women of China, and the semi-independent New World section. A lively FLP quartet (C. D. Alison Bailey, Carole Murray, Don Cohn, and Jon von Kowallis)[7] also celebrated my fortieth birthday with me.

Meanwhile, the world outside China was beginning to appreciate the direction in which China seemed to be going in the early 1980s. A constant stream of invitations arrived from Europe (then including Britain), the US, and Australia to publish translations from contemporary Chinese poetry and fiction, especially by women, that I was only too eager to accept. It was sheer coincidence, nevertheless, that just at this time I happened to meet one of the most outstanding writers of the post-Mao period.

***

In October 1982, my contract had been renewed for one year and my income increased to RMB$750 per month. A year later, when my contract from the previous year expired, I was surprised that the FLP decided not to offer another renewal. But I likely shouldn't have been. By that time, my translations of dissident poetry and fiction had been published abroad. An FLP editor whose poetry I had begun to translate independently had already been warned not to waste my highly paid time during office hours. It was determined that I should not only be refused an extension to my contract but should also be prevented from being employed elsewhere. My approaches to a handful of universities around Beijing were at first welcomed, but a day or so later I would get a message that after all there were no vacancies in their institution; one professor told me in a whisper that the FLP had let them know that I "knew too many people." Eventually, an institution known to have "right-wing tendencies" hired me, and I spent another year and a half in Beijing.

My ostracization was not stringently observed within the FLP, and I remained a casual contributor to FLP publications until the end of the century. Throughout this period, my role was in many ways privileged: I was usually on good terms with my fellow translators but rarely had contact with their seniors, with the notable exception of Gladys Yang and Yang Xianyi. Gladys had a large group of close friends, with many young women like Carole Murray and Alison Bailey, and to some extent I was also included. I recall, for instance, that she introduced me to the popular novelist Dick Francis, warning me that I should be prepared to think well of horses. After I'd left China, between 1986 and 1990, Gladys's letters were a treasured source of news and gossip; Xianyi wrote only rarely.[8]

In 1989 Xianyi abandoned his distanced stand in regard to current political affairs and spoke out against the violent suppression of the protest movement centered on Tiananmen Square. This was done at great personal danger, but in 1990 he was able to resume a more normal life but without his former insouciance. Gladys died in 1999; I was honored to be a contributor to the British Library's Gladys Yang: Memorial Book and Archive the following year. I continued to see Xianyi whenever I could make a visit to Beijing, which became easier once I'd moved to Hong Kong. At first, he was sent to live in a small, cramped apartment far off in the southwestern district, far from where his friends and supporters could easily visit, but after a year or so his salary and savings were restored, and he was able to move into an elegant, old-fashioned house near Back Lake in central Beijing. His daughter and her husband moved in as well and looked after him. Before long, however, his health deteriorated, and he became too weak to receive visitors or even move without help. A grand funeral in 2009 was held for him at the cemetery reserved for the country's most distinguished citizens. I admired both Xianyi and Gladys beyond reason: they were my heroes, personally and professionally, during my time at the FLP. Up until the start of the global pandemic in 2019, I also managed to keep in touch with a few of the junior staff who had by the turn of the century been promoted for their talent and dedication; several have remained active even in retirement.

As far as I was personally involved, in-house or casual translation by any Chinese institution in the early 1980s was neither wholly voluntary nor wholly commercial but often somewhere in between. As far as I was concerned, however, I always chose payment, and in no sense can my translations be characterized as gifts that I was preparing for the world or any part thereof. The FLP itself has since changed enormously and mostly for the better. I look back on those days with embarrassment and nostalgia.

Notes

1. The poems were published in *Renmin wenxue* in 1961.
2. Hu Feng was the pen name of Zhang Mingzhen (1902–1985), who dissented from Mao's views on literature and was jailed in 1955. When he was released in 1979, he was in poor mental and physical health. His essays disputing Mao's views were republished in 1984.
3. *Nagel's Encyclopedia-Guide: China* (Nagel Publishers: Geneva, 1968).
4. McDougall, "Censorship & Self-Censorship in Contemporary Chinese Literature."
5. Gerber and Qi, eds., *A Century of Chinese Literature in Translation (1919–2019)*.
6. See also Perry Link, ed., *Stubborn Weeds: Popular and Controversial Chinese Literature after the Cultural Revolution* (Bloomington: Indiana University Press, 1983), 194–197. There's a misprint on page 196: "member" should be "mender."
7. C. D. Alison Bailey later became an assistant professor of Chinese at the University of British Columbia; Jon von Kowallis is a professor of Chinese at the University of New South Wales; Carole Murray embarked on a legal career; and Don Cohn writes about aspects of Chinese culture and society and sells antiquarian books.
8. To some extent my respect and affection for Gladys and Xianyi Yang are represented in McDougall, "Intuition and Spontaneity in Multiple Voice Literary Translation."

CHAPTER 7

SHADOWS POETRY AND FICTION

While I was working for the FLP and later for the College of Foreign Affairs, I was also getting to know young writers (and a few film directors) who were involved in controversial new movements. As mentioned earlier, I had started to take an interest in "unofficial" Chinese literature during my summer in Hong Kong in 1978. My appointment at the FLP had come almost two decades after I'd first lived in China, and although my understanding of written Chinese had improved, I'd lost fluency in spoken Chinese. At the FLP, I wrestled daily with written Chinese but spoke mainly English. Now that I was living in China, it was thanks to this new unofficial literature that I gradually became familiar again with spoken Chinese. My home-based translations of this new poetry and fiction, however, still drew on the formalities of written Chinese, and my English was similarly bookish. Were I to translate again the poems from the 1970s and early 1980s, the main subject of this chapter, I imagine that my English would be different but not dramatically so, though, because the poems themselves had a certain formality.

The early 1980s saw a truly remarkable upsurge outside China of translations of new Chinese poetry and fiction. Although later official accounts of these works describe them as a post–Cultural Revolution phenomenon, the new wave had its origins during the social chaos of the early 1970s. Despite efforts of the Party elite, a state of near anarchy prevailed beyond their control. Bizarre as it now seems, young people were able to defy the repression of the times by turning to writing and distributing hand-written copies of their own fiction and poetry.

From late 1978 and most of the following year, crowds of mainly young people gathered at Xidan in central Beijing and put up "big-character posters" on what became known as the "Democracy Wall." As well as protesting about political and social issues, some of them also posted new poetry and fiction; the former soon became famous throughout China as "obscure poetry." This material gained a wider audience through mimeographed journals of what was called "unofficial writing." Young activists "borrowed" paper, ink, and copier machines from their friends and relatives working in offices in big and small cities and towns throughout China to circulate on a wider scale the underground literature of the previous years. Easy to memorize, poetry was the most convenient form for widespread circulation; short fiction was also popular, and eventually full-length novels were able to break through official censorship.

It was during this time that I first met Bei Dao. He Qifang was my link to Bei Dao, improbable as it still seems. In 1981 I received a letter from a young Chinese woman living in north China who had read *Paths in Dreams* (or at least had seen and been intrigued by its cover). She had written to me care of University of Queensland Press under her nom de plume "Amelia," but her letter only reached me after we'd moved to China. A student of both English and contemporary Chinese poetry, she'd read and translated poems by Walt Whitman, Emily Dickinson, James Joyce, Oscar Wilde, and Sylvia Plath, an unexpectedly generous list for the time, and some of her own poems had appeared in print. (Later we learned that like Zhu Guangqian, she'd read that I was a well-known short-story writer and my husband was a literary critic. I wonder how many people, besides these two, had read this misinformation).

Shadows Poetry and Fiction

On a visit to Harbin in 1982, we met Amelia and her fiancé Cao Changqing, a poet and journalist who now lives in the US. Because his work allowed him to travel regularly to Beijing, he offered to introduce us to "the best new poet in China." Cao and Bei Dao arrived at our small flat on June 2. Later the same month, we met Shao Fei, Bei Dao's wife, and the younger poet Gu Cheng; we met Chen Maiping in October. The pattern for our close friendship with Bei Dao, Shao Fei, and Chen Maiping, along with many others, was now set. Bei Dao and his companions, it must be stressed, did not become influential in China because of me or any other foreigner. Their poems, written and circulating since the early 1970s, had achieved an enthusiastic readership throughout China, and at the time most recently from their posting on Beijing's Democracy Wall.[1]

For our first meeting, Bei Dao had brought along handwritten copies of some of his best-known poems, and that night I began to translate them. I was immediately captivated and continued to work on these poems until late. The only problem was how and where to contact him again and come to some arrangement about translating and publishing his poems. In the early 1980s, unofficial visits to the Friendship Hotel were forbidden to Chinese people, although it was relatively easy to evade surveillance (by arriving in a taxi, for instance). However, it so happened that Bei Dao was an editor at the FLP's Esperanto section, and this fortunate coincidence of sharing a workplace allowed us to communicate freely for about a year, after which complaints were made, and our personal contact became more complicated. Sometimes we'd have a picnic at the Yuanmingyuan, taking our son with us and meeting some of the other young poets; occasionally we'd meet at the Beijing Zoo, where Torkel took alarm at the rhinoceros. One longish excursion was to a scenic spot in the countryside for which a bus was hired, although a jealous altercation between two Chinese men and an American woman onboard caused the driver to lose his temper. Sometimes a social outing was just for our two families: Bei Dao and Shao Fei, Anders and me. Taking advantage of winter gloom that kept people inside and dictated heavy padded coats for excursions outside, we visited Bei Dao's cramped shack where later we had the pleasure of holding their first baby; there was no running water or lavatory in their two tiny rooms, but they did at least have neighbors who left them alone.

A few months later, the political climate began to show signs of reverting to the bad old days. It suddenly seemed essential to make every effort to introduce Bei Dao's work to sinologists who might translate and publicize it. These efforts had already started with Wolfgang Kubin, a dedicated sinologist, translator, and poet who soon became one of Bei Dao's close friends. By 1983 the list of visitors had rapidly increased: they included the professor of Chinese at Stockholm University Göran Malmqvist, who also came to play a huge part in Bei Dao's life. The onset of the 1983 campaign against the absurdly named "spiritual pollution" became increasingly threatening up to its open declaration in October.[2] The campaign included named attacks in the national press on individual young writers, making it imperative to protect not only Bei Dao's work but also the writer himself and his family.

The situation compelled us to try publishing abroad rather than introduce them to foreigners visiting China. We discussed how we could best launch an international appeal in the likely event of Bei Dao's arrest and imprisonment and how we could protect his wife and baby daughter (thankfully, it never came to this): publishing translations of his work in English and other languages became a crucial part of the solution. Within a few weeks, I was preparing the first ever book-length collection of Bei Dao's poetry to appear in any language, as well as sending individual poems abroad. Thanks to prompt action by Edward Gunn, a friend I'd met during our Harvard years, this book was published by the Cornell University China-Japan Program in 1983 under the title *Notes from the City of the Sun: Poems by Bei Dao*; a revised edition appeared the following year. As far as I can remember, neither Bei Dao nor I received a fee or royalties, in order to keep the cost down, but I'm afraid I don't have any paperwork to confirm this. In any case, I promptly ordered dozens of copies and devised ways of receiving and distributing them in China as well as to interested parties abroad. The translations in this selection of Bei Dao's poems from the 1970s to 1983 were drawn from copies handwritten expressly for this volume, the author's original manuscripts, or published versions that had appeared in unofficial or other relatively obscure publications. The book was designed to be low cost and to include the original Chinese so that it could reach readers in China.

My translations of Bei Dao's poem were also published in *Renditions*, the leading international journal of Chinese literature in English translation, founded in 1973 in Hong Kong by Chinese American author, translator, and journalist George Kao (1912–2008) and prolific writer and translator Stephen Soong (1919–1996). My first contribution to it was sent from Harvard and published in 1978.[3] Otherwise, most of the translations I made in the late 1970s appeared in the modest 1980–1981 issue of *Modern Chinese Literature Newsletter*. It was largely due to British sinologist and literary translator John Minford, the then new *Renditions* editor, that I became more involved in the journal. A brilliant translator himself, Minford was also an innovative editor, actively seeking out new authors and translators. *Renditions* became an ideal venue for new poetry and film and commanded my whole attention for the first half of the 1980s. We'd met John Minford in Beijing in 1984 and in the same year visited him in Hong Kong, where our encounters at the Chinese University of Hong Kong (CUHK) sealed our cooperation. My first submission was fifteen poems by Bei Dao in a special issue on contemporary Chinese literature,[4] along with the short stories "Waves" ("Bodong" 波动) and "Moon on the Manuscript" ("Gaozhi shang de yueliang" 稿纸上的月亮).[5] This issue was reprinted as *Trees on the Mountain*, edited by Stephen C. Soong and John Minford.[6] In the following year I sent *Renditions* thirteen lyric poems by Zhu Xiang[7]; the issue containing these poems was reprinted as *A Brotherhood of Song*, also edited by Stephen C. Soong and John Minford in 1985. Ten poems by Bei Dao then appeared in the next issue of *Renditions*,[8] and his last short story, "Thirteen Happiness Street" ("Xingfu dajie shisan hao" 幸福大街十三号) in the issue that followed.[9]

The campaign against spiritual pollution collapsed early in 1984, by which time Bei Dao's fame had spread ever more widely across China, and translations of his poems for publication abroad had steadily increased. Requests for interviews with him and invitations to travel abroad became bewilderingly many. Starting from 1984, Bei Dao became the first twentieth-century Chinese poet to achieve a worldwide audience; only Mao Zedong could claim more readers.

The path to this worldwide audience was not without its challenges, as I note in my introductory essay, "A Poetry of Shadows: An Introduction to Bei Dao's Poems" (dated December 1982), in *Notes from the City of the Sun*, whose main content consists of forty-one poems Bei Dao and I had selected and his manifesto "About Poetry." The Chinese versions of the poems and manifesto follow the translations and were written, at Bei Dao's request, by a pen rather than by a brush.

One of the issues raised in the introduction is the translation of the phrase *menglong shi* 朦胧诗: my preferred translation, then and now, is "a poetry of shadows," abbreviated as "shadows poetry/poems." The term *menglong* consists of two characters, each written with the moon radical, that describe the dim light shed by the moon at night. The addition of the word *shi*, meaning poetry, conveys at least two distinct messages in this context: that the meaning of the poetry itself is obscure, not openly declaring its inner significance (unlike the declamatory manner of the official literature) and that it is strikingly opposed to the Chinese mainstream, with the symbol of the moon itself as obverse to the sun, which was still dominant in Chinese literature, art, and politics. Further expanding the term, *menglong shiren* was translated to "shadows poet" ("shady poet" would have been disastrous). Initially, the common translation of *menglong shi* was "obscure poetry," appropriate enough but clumsy, the main problem being the corresponding term "obscure poet," a description which by this time was rapidly becoming out of date. (A newspaper cartoon at the time showed an emcee standing by a microphone introducing "an obscure poet" who appeared as a mass of short pen strokes, unidentifiable as a living human being.[10]) Within a few years, another translation emerged that soon became dominant: "misty poetry" and "misty poet." I still consider this an unfortunate choice: the original expression describes a quality of light, not of water, and the word "mist" as a symbol conveys little sense of purposely concealed meaning and significance. In any case, these variations around the mid-1980s point to the rapidly increasing prestige that new-wave poetry was achieving in popular culture: shadows poetry was becoming an acceptable addition to literary magazines around the country.

Over the course of the next few weeks, I encountered technical matters similar to those I'd found in translating He Qifang's poems. One obvious question concerned rhyme, whether rhymed verse in one language should be rhymed in translation, and if so, whether the two rhyme schemes should be identical. The kind of sectional, irregular verse that featured prominently in Bei Dao's early poems, represented by "Notes from the City of the Sun," is a distinct departure from conventional post-1949 Chinese verse that is largely rhymed. The absence of conventional rhyme schemes in these poems underlines the experimental and unconventional structure of the poems as a whole. Additionally, the tone of the structurally conventional poems can be distinguished from the tone of the structurally unconventional poems. Thus, the tone of "The Answer" ("Huida" 回答) is relatively direct, concrete, and even strident, whereas "Notes from the City of the Sun" ("Taiyang cheng zhaji" 太阳城札記) is indirect, abstract, and muffled.

Rhyme in translation is difficult to do well, but it can enhance the difference between different groups of poems, regardless of its use in the original poems. Contemporary practice tends to avoid rhyme in translating poetry into English. Nevertheless, I'd already come across two cases where it seemed appropriate, in poems by Qiu Xiaolong and by the May Fourth poet Zhu Xiang.[11] For the latter's poem "Nocturne" ("Ciye ti" 雌夜啼), I adopted a standard English rhyme pattern, including some half-rhymes as in the original. The reason for adopting rhyme here over a more literal meaning is that the poem creates a general mood rather than describing actual scenes or events. Because rhyme was clearly a factor in the poet's own choice of words, the translator would be justified in adopting the same criterion: an unrhymed translation might even be considered inadequate. I'd previously experimented with formal rhyme in translating pseudo-folk songs from the Cultural Revolution, but Zhu Xiang's poems from the 1930s offered more genuine engagement. It was also an agreeable return to the tradition of dead poets.

Otherwise, I tried to avoid rhyme, whether or not it existed in the poems I was translating, by adopting a technique used in English (and to some extent also in other European languages): replacing the initial capital letter for the first word in each line with a lowercase letter. Although this technique is now over a century old in English, it still conveys a sense of modernity that is appropriate for translations of late twentieth-century poetry in China.[12]

***

While preparations for *Notes from the City of the Sun* were still underway, my translations and co-translations of poetry and fiction by Bei Dao and his contemporaries had begun to appear in magazines in the English-speaking world, most notably in *Renditions*, which has been a major part of my life as a literary translator. My first contribution, the short story "Smoke Shadows" ("Yan ying" 烟影) by Yu Dafu, appeared in spring 1978 when Stephen C. Soong was executive editor. For it I received the splendid sum of US$340 and four copies of the translation. Grateful for the publishers' generosity, I began to subscribe to the journal itself. The following year I submitted a few poems by He Jingzhi (no relation to He Qifang), to which Stephen C. Soong sent a long and utterly persuasive letter to explain the reasons for its rejection.

Around 1983, John Minford took over as editor, with Don Cohn (who had been a good friend since both of us worked for the FLP) as his assistant, and thereafter for several years *Renditions* became the home for my translation efforts, especially for Bei Dao and Wan Zhi (the penname of Chen Maiping). I'd met John on his visit to Beijing just after he'd succeeded Stephen C. Soong, and he immediately became an enthusiastic supporter of shadows poetry. The *Renditions* Special Issue on Chinese Literature Today, dated spring and autumn 1983 (its actual appearance was in early 1984) featured both poetry and fiction by Bei Dao, among others; it was augmented and republished in 1984 as a Renditions Book under the title *Trees on the Mountain: An Anthology of New Chinese Writing*.[13] *Trees on the Mountain* is still in print at The Chinese University Press. I've greatly admired John's translations, and although I've always been more cautious, perhaps under his influence I became a little more relaxed and open to experiment.

***

While at Harvard, I'd translated a handful of officially released poems from the early 1970s; later, following a visit to Hong Kong in 1976, I'd also translated and written about the new poetry and fiction then gradually appearing on the mainland and being given wider publicity in Hong Kong. Known as "scar literature," this effusion of anger and hope was bracing but not in itself immediately able to establish new standards for a more nuanced literary movement. It wasn't until I began reading poetry and fiction by Bei Dao and his fellow "obscure" writers, however, that I began to appreciate this truly exciting new literary movement. The rest of my time at the Foreign Languages Press was spent translating old hacks such as Guo Moruo during the daylight hours and returning to the Friendship Hotel in the evening eager to translate into English the most authentic Chinese poetry I'd read since the days of Wen Yiduo, Xu Zhimo, Bian Zhilin, and He Qifang.

In the aftermath of the "spiritual pollution" crisis of 1983, foreigners in China found it easier to meet Chinese writers. Despite his frequent plunges into depression, Bei Dao was part of a lively social group that included both locals and foreigners. Shao Fei was a talented painter and daughter of a more famous mother; her paintings changed dramatically during the 1980s as she developed her own style, a process that can be seen over the years on the dust jackets of her husband's later collections. The writers in this group included Gu Cheng, Yang Lian, Duo Duo, and the ever-loyal Chen Maiping, who remained a close friend throughout the years. Our relations with older writers were more distant or only took place by written correspondence; these writers included Zou Difan, Zheng Min, Luo Gengye, Lu Li, Liu Gangshan, Wang Erbei, and Bai Hong.

Gu Cheng was one of the most agreeable of our new friends, and it seemed also that Bei Dao was impressed by his work but concerned about his vulnerability. Gu Cheng was usually mild and gentle, and he was also the only one in the loosely formed group who showed interest in places and events outside of China. Some of his poems seemed a bit too simple, as if he were begging for people to like them and him. I translated only three of his poems[14] since there were plenty of other translators pressing to translate his work. The one I liked best was about a buried flagon of Shaoxing wine excavated to celebrate a wedding. Later, what seemed at first to be pretenses at being weirdly unconventional gave way to actual descents into madness, which only his wife Xie Ye, also a poet, could assuage, and only for some time. His shocking murder of his wife and suicide on a chicken farm in New Zealand years later was a horrible end to two lives that seemed to hold infinite promise.

Younger and more ambitious writers also introduced themselves to us. There was no mistaking that as they sought translation, they regarded translators themselves as a necessary go-between to a world of fame and fortune. I grew tired of strange young men accosting me with sheaves of papers in their hands during walks at the Summer Palace (Yiheyuan) or at the Yuanmingyuan or even knocking on my door (that was only possible after I later moved to the College of Foreign Affairs, now known as China Foreign Affairs University). I was even less impressed by the efforts of some writers to seduce me (romantically paired Chinese-foreign translation partnerships had become commonplace by the mid-1980s).

Certainly, many writers wished to leave China on wholly reasonable grounds, but it wasn't my role as translator to help them realize their ambitions. Older, native translators, in contrast and unsurprisingly, tended to be dismissive of foreign translators.[15]

Even in those urgently political years I hadn't altogether deserted the poets of the 1930s: *Renditions* published my translation of thirteen lyric poems by Zhu Xiang in the Special Issue on Poetry and Poetics of 1983 and reprinted in *A Brotherhood of Song* in 1985. Zhu Xiang had died young, but the poems he left behind were a joy to read and translate. For these I had no need to ask for help: the literal meanings were transparent, even if the sentiment was elusive. Given conditions in China at this time, I felt no obligation to make these subtleties explicit.

***

The first book collection of Bei Dao's fiction in any language was *Waves: Stories by Zhao Zhenkai*. The translations of the six short stories in the first edition were shared between Susette Ternent Cooke and me; I acted as editor and wrote an introduction. The collection was first published by The Chinese University Press in Hong Kong in 1985. The first print run of a thousand copies sold out in a few months, and a revised and expanded edition appeared the following year and sold another thousand copies.

By the end of the 1970s, Bei Dao was able to circulate more widely the short fiction he'd been writing since 1972. His first, longest, and most notable work of fiction was the novella "Waves,"[16] which was followed by six shorter works, all of which were based on real people and events. The stories "In the Ruins" ("Feixu shang" 廢墟上) and "The Homecoming Stranger" ("Guilai de moshengren" 歸來的陌生人) were written expressly for the first and second issue of the unofficial journal *Jintian* (Today) of which Bei Dao was coeditor. The next three, "Melody" ("Xuanlü" 旋律), "Moon on the Manuscript," and "Intersection" ("Jiaochadian" 交叉點) appeared in the official journals of the early 1980s. The last story,

"Thirteen Happiness Street," which was added in the revised edition, has the most disturbing title with its promise of betrayal.

It was probably a mistake to choose Bei Dao's legal name, Zhao Zhenkai, when it came to publishing his fiction: I had some notion of separating the two very different bodies of work. A British edition of *Waves* published in 1987 changed the name of the author to Bei Dao, who had by now reached international audiences under his pen name as a poet. This edition was followed by a paperback in 1989 and a revised North American edition in 1990. Each of these publications, to the best of my recollections, yielded royalties for all three of us. By this time, translations into European languages as well as Japanese made Bei Dao a world-famous figure who acted as a spokesperson for political and cultural change in China and singled out to be a strong candidate for the Nobel Prize for Literature. To date, this honor has eluded him, but many other foundations and universities around the world have continued to recognize his international standing. The Hong Kong editions of *Waves* in English and in Chinese published by CUHK in the 1980s were not the last step that formed a bond between Bei Dao and the Chinese University of Hong Kong, where the writer eventually took up full-time residence following years of travel in Europe and America. Works by Bei Dao and his colleagues now form an official archive of the CUHK Library, where most of his early manuscripts are lodged and digitized.

***

The novella "Waves" is one of the most innovative and ambitious stories of 1970s China in narrative technique, moral sensitivity, and social understanding. The cast of five characters range from a young woman whose parents committed suicide as persecuted intellectuals and whose own illegitimate daughter has been deserted by her father; her new lover, a slightly selfish, spoiled young man from a high-ranking family based in Beijing; a middle-aged provincial official who is also an old comrade-in-arms and the former lover of the young man's mother; a violent, ruthless, and promiscuous young hooligan who nevertheless retains a sense of justice and pity for the innocent; and the official's frustrated daughter, who falls hopelessly in love with the young man. Each is given the role of narrator in successive episodes. These narrators are supplemented by a host of secondary characters.

The result of this complex narrative was a significant breakthrough in PRC literature in both form and content. The plot, to a large extent revisiting the lives of people known to the author, evokes the day-to-day lives of educated young and older Chinese men and women struggling to survive in 1970s China. Underlining a physical manifestation of the narrators' search for meaning in life, they seem always to be traveling, mainly by train, and a significant part of the action takes place in railway or bus station waiting rooms. The introduction of a new character archetype to post-1949 fiction, the petty criminal and a former educated youth (*zhishi qingnian* 知识青年, or "sent-down" youth[17]), exposes the extent of corruption and criminality in Cultural Revolution China. Another innovative feature is the treatment of death: in "Waves" it is not the glorious fate of the hero, nor the contemptible fate of the villain, nor even the pathetic fate of the middle characters, but a human tragedy shattering the lives of the survivors. Then there is the love affair between the two main characters, as well as open references to sexuality among several of the other characters, showing a sensitivity to the emotional turmoil that had been missing in Chinese fiction since the 1940s.

"In the Ruins" and "The Homecoming Stranger" are set in the years shortly after the end of the Cultural Revolution, dwelling on the suffering experienced during those years in urban professional and domestic life, somewhat lightened by a belief that society and the individual can be reconciled. "Melody," the most sentimental of these stories, was written and published in 1980, when the characters' most personal and intimate matters, from housing to divorce, are still in the unforgiving hands of bureaucrats, intensifying problems in already troubled marriages. More detached from Bei Dao is the protagonist of "Moon on the Manuscript":

the literature professor's students reject his lectures; his wife is oblivious to all but the mundane details of their shared life; and an old, high-status couple promise to publish his work, in an example of corrupt literary patronage and plagiarism; bureaucratic injustice and cultural poverty were still features of life in post–Cultural Revolution China. "Intersection" is an appealing account of an encounter in a local bar between a worker and an engineer, both employed at a nearby construction site. During that period, the two characters, an uneducated worker and a tertiary-educated professional, would ordinarily have no social contact. When this unlikely meeting happens, the worker is already half drunk and the engineer is in despair about his home life. The more they drink, the more relaxed they become; and when the bar closes, they stagger out under the dim streetlights. As they walk away they began to sing, their voices drifting as they sing of life's vicissitudes and of friendship. The next morning, when their paths cross, they are silent. In seven short pages, the author depicts the barely concealed aggression of class hostility in China during the 1970s, which is far removed from the manufactured idylls lauded by the ruling clique and their followers. The last story "Thirteen Happiness Street" has an even more subversive theme: a mordant Kafkaesque tale of a young boy's disappearance.

Bei Dao's fiction has attracted less attention than his poetry, if only because he has not continued to write and publish in this mode. It is also the case that his technical breakthroughs are now commonplace and that twenty-first-century readers are no longer in need of enlightenment about Cultural Revolution–era China and its aftermath. Nevertheless, the stories still merit attention: a revival of popular interest in them is long overdue. In contrast, my translation of Mao Zedong's "Talks" has attracted academic readers, but it is far outweighed by requests for republication of Bei Dao's poems I translated for the collection *The August Sleepwalker* and its successors, as well as questions and interviews about my poetry translations.

Shadows Poetry and Fiction

***

Another new step for me in the mid-1980s was an occasional foray into interpreting, from Chinese to English and back. This was due mainly to the increasing number of visitors to Beijing from outside China in the mid-1980s and similarly increasing numbers of Chinese people traveling abroad. The most rewarding encounter I can now recall was the visit of a group of American writers to China at the invitation of the Chinese Writers Association. At the compulsory opening banquet, I was introduced to American poets Allen Ginsberg and Gary Snyder, who both expressed an interest in Bei Dao and his work. Bei Dao was still not a member of the Chinese Writers Association, and none of the Chinese writers were scheduled to meet the visitors, but Ginsberg had heard about Bei Dao and was keen to meet him. I arranged a private meeting between Ginsberg, Snyder, and Bei Dao in which I acted as their interpreter, and the three men developed a good rapport. Right at the beginning, however, I made a stupid error. With his customary courtesy, Bei Dao started by mentioning Ginsberg's most famous poem, saying it had made a deep impression on him; caught up in the moment, I translated the title to Ginsberg as "The Roar," only to be corrected immediately by him. Toward the end of the conversation, Bei Dao was startled to hear from Ginsberg that he was an ardent Buddhist but quickly recovered and listened politely as Ginsberg related his personal interpretation of Buddhism and how it affected his life and writing.

Following my departure from the FLP, I was struck by the relatively benign indifference of the College of Foreign Affairs regarding my extracurricular activities. The college was generally regarded as rightist, thanks to its parent, China's Foreign Ministry. One of my former colleagues at the FLP kindly persuaded a family member at the college to have me recruited there as a translation teacher. As with most educational institutions, living quarters were provided on campus. In most respects, the standards were significantly lower than at the Friendship Hotel (for instance, getting milk meant having to queue up around 5:30 in the morning). Still there was one huge improvement: while there was a guard post at the main gates, Chinese visitors were only cursorily asked to provide IDs; in addition, there was a constant sizable hole in the fencing around the campus near our living quarters that allowed easy entry and exit despite repeated attempts by the authorities to mend it.

Within China and among other scholars of modern Chinese literature, my record as the translator of China's most outstanding poet, fiction writer (see chapter 10) and film director (see chapter 8) of the mid-1980s was an immense satisfaction to me. As I was learning to write for a wider audience, my confidence grew accordingly. Although I wasn't aware of it at the time, translation was beginning to rule my life.

Now long retired, I wonder why exactly I chose to spend at least three to four years living in (and thereafter visiting almost annually) the country whose language I'd already spent most of my life studying, and to work for a government-operated firm whose direction was in line with official policies. This choice could be regarded as stemming from both cynical opportunism and a misguided belief in my own righteous wish to contribute to a dynamic new interpretation about what it means to be and speak Chinese.

It may seem both inevitable and desirable that a translator would wish to spend lengthy periods in the country where her foreign language is dominant, especially when her home and foreign cultures lie far apart. Not everyone would agree with even this simple proposition. My university supervisor, whose views influenced me greatly when I was a student in Sydney, made a point of not going to China (although under pressure he undertook a single brief trip): he felt the translator's native language should be kept uncontaminated. I have some sympathy with this view. Some years earlier, I'd stopped reading translated literature in order to avoid drifting toward a foreignized version of English. (I now understand this might be a quite stupid move.) Nevertheless, I'd become conscious that it had been many years since I'd been fluent in spoken Chinese, and I wished to recover my earlier proficiency. Once back in China in 1980, I found a tutor for spoken Chinese without bothering about whether my English would thereafter be contaminated.

Another major factor in choosing China as our next location after Cambridge was the availability of trouble-free childcare. Otherwise, my main motivation for being in China was that the political situation, and by extension the literary world, was undergoing extensive and rapid change, and I was both curious and impressed. As for earning a living, my employment skills were limited to teaching and translation; I had taught but had no experience of being a paid translator. Even my awful memories of having lived in China in the past had been fading with the conviction that everything was changing; I was taking a second chance on China when I went in the early 1980s. In the end, spending a couple of years in China, compared with trying to get a job in the US or any other country, seemed vaguely attractive. In other words, I understood very little about the consequences of this move or how long it would be. As for my activities in these years as a Chinese government employee, I'd veered between taking a preachy reformist stance toward a country emerging from a long crisis and having the nagging sense of being a crusading colonial subject and arrogant colonial oppressor. This dilemma took some time to resolve.

Notes

1. From late 1978 and for most of the following year, crowds of mainly young people gathered at Xidan in central Beijing and put up "big-character posters" on what became known as the "Democracy Wall." As well as protesting about political and social issues, some of them also posted their new poetry and fiction; the former soon became famous throughout China as "obscure poetry."
2. The foreign staff in other parts of the FLP sought to find a more acceptable English translation for the Chinese term *jingshen wuran* 精神污染; I recall that one of them was "cultural contamination."
3. Yu Ta-fu, "Smoke Shadows." For some years, the date of *Renditions* printing was only a rough guide to the date of actual production.
4. *Renditions* 19 and 20 (Spring and Autumn 1983): 195–208.
5. *Renditions* 19 and 20 (Spring and Autumn 1983):125–167 and 173–178. The author was given as Zhao Zhenkai.
6. Pagination was identical to the journal issue.
7. This was for the special issue 21 and 22 (Spring and Autumn 1984; actual publication was probably in 1985).
8. *Renditions* 23 (Spring 1985): 111–116.
9. *Renditions* 24 (Autumn 1985): 3–12.
10. The cartoon is reprinted in *Trees on the Mountain*, 184.
11. Thirteen lyric poems by Chu Hsiang [Zhu Xiang].
12. As described in my article "Problems and Possibilities in Translating Contemporary Chinese Literature."
13. See fifteen poems by Bei Dao in Special Issue on Chinese Literature Today; Zhao Zhenkai, "Moon on the Manuscript"; Ten poems by Bei Dao; Bei Dao, "Thirteen Happiness Street," 5–12, 173–178.
14. "Three Poems by Gu Cheng."
15. See McDougall, "Intuition and Spontaneity in Multiple Voice Literary Translation."
16. 1974; revised versions 1976, 1979, 1981, and 1984.
17. "Educated youth" are urban Chinese youth who were sent by the government to the countryside for reeducation during the Cultural Revolution.

Part IV

Oslo and Edinburgh

Chapter 8

Spoken and Unspoken Words

Much of any play or film is its performance; so how can the translation of the script alone ever do it justice? Adding to this issue is the fact that in drama and film, especially the latter, the author's autocratic position is illusory. At the top of a pyramid stands the director, and even if the script has been circulated in advance, it is just a nonbinding guide to what the play or film will actually become. On what should translators rely, the script, drama, or film? The choice isn't necessarily theirs to make. I'd avoided translating plays, the only exception being one of the popular playwright Ding Xilin's short works. I've been a fan of Ding Xilin's short, witty, and enlightened plays since the 1980s: I'd introduced his play *A Wasp* (*Yi zhi mafeng* 精神污染一只马蜂) to my Oslo classes in 1986,[1] and my co-translation of *Dear Husband* (*Qin'ai de zhangfu* 亲爱的丈夫), appeared in *Renditions* in 1999. I'd also avoided translating film, although as a personal favor I agreed to translate the script of the 1983 film version of Jiang Zilong's *All the Colors of the Rainbow* (*Chi cheng huang lü qing lan zi* 赤橙黄绿青蓝紫). My request to watch the film itself was met with surprise mixed with hostility; obtaining the film seemed as if it was never going to be easy, and it never was. The film was released in 1982 and dropped out of sight a year or two later.

Undeterred, I decided to translate Chen Kaige's *The Yellow Earth* (*Huang tudi* 黄土地) in autumn 1982, before the film itself had started production. Chen Kaige is now best known for two outstanding works: his first full-length feature film *The Yellow Earth* from 1984, and the equally remarkable *Farewell My Concubine* (*Ba wang bie ji* 霸王別姬), based on the novel of the same name, from 1993. I've still only the faintest knowledge of film production or reception but have never doubted that *The Yellow Earth* remains one of the most extraordinary and significant Chinese films ever made.

***

The story of my involvement with Chen Kaige and a few of his early films proved to be much longer and more complicated than I'd expected. It begins with Bei Dao asking if I would be willing to coach the wife of one of his friends because she was about to study abroad and wanted to improve her English; I agreed. Her name was Sun Jialin, and she was an engineer about to leave for Canada to study solar-panel engineering. Her husband, Chen Kaige, was an assistant film director who also wanted to improve his beginner's knowledge of English. Bei Dao and Chen Maiping were also keen on improving their grasp of English. We all met in the bedroom of the small flat Chen and his wife shared with his parents in the Beijing Film Studio compound, where his father was a senior film director and his mother a senior scriptwriter and CCP member. Many years later I discovered that Sun Jialin's mother was a student of Gladys Yang's during her Nanking teaching days. I continued to correspond with Sun Jialin while she was in Canada until the end of the 1980s.

Chen Kaige had attended the same elite high school as Bei Dao (who was two years his senior), and they'd stayed in touch in the early post–Cultural Revolution period. In 1980, under the pen name Xia Ge, Chen Kaige contributed the short story "The Masked Dance" ("Jiamian wuhui" 假面舞会) in *Jintian*. Chen Kaige's story revolved around the awkward behavior of a young man at a dance party of the kind that had suddenly become popular in the capital; the writer himself appears to share qualities of both the clumsy dancer and the sophisticated fellow student who observes the dancer's behavior and narrates the story. I found the work subtle and persuasive and translated it for publication in an international Swiss-based literary journal *2PLUS2* in 1986. For this I received US$150, most of which I handed over to Chen Kaige when I next saw him.[2]

Our English classes were informal: opinions on literary matters led to animated discussion. Among our readings, I recall William Blake's poems most clearly. After class, I would perch on the back of Chen Kaige's bike as he returned me to the Friendship Hotel. Classes continued for a couple of years, with attendance and composition changing over the months. For the most part, it was an exhilarating experience. It also led to Chen Kaige entrusting me with early scripts of *The Yellow Earth*.

The film's origins at first had not been promising. Based on a short essay by Ke Lan, a screenplay was first drafted by Zhang Ziliang, who at the time was working as a scriptwriter at the Xi'an Film Studio. The studio was not interested in it, but Zhang Yimou, a fellow student of Chen Kaige's at the Beijing Film Academy, who was specializing in cinematography and from Xi'an, thought it showed promise and passed it on to Chen Kaige at the Beijing Film Studio. The Beijing Film Studio was the country's most famous studio, lavishly equipped with a budget allowing twenty films a year and seventy directors on staff. It was an exceptional opportunity for Chen Kaige to prove his worth with his first studio film as a full director (he'd previously directed two television dramas). Once approved, he set about recruiting his staff (including Zhang Yimou) and working on the script, dividing his time between Shaanxi and Beijing.

By early 1983, I'd completed a rough draft translation of *The Yellow Earth*'s "literary script" but was unhappy with its verbosity and apparent distance from the film itself, which by this time I had seen in an early version screened in an army compound. Instead, I pestered the director for a copy of the *taiben* 台本, the tabulated (i.e., working) script or a dialogue-based playscript since it would not only be a better guide to the film itself but also superior as literature in its more concise formulations of plot, characterization, and descriptions of the settings. This working script was in the form of a mimeographed copy lent to me by the director with his own corrections clearly visible. Chen Kaige and Chen Maiping (who was responsible for drafting the script) were among my advisors on matters beyond my reach. My translation was completed in 1986; it was further revised for the published version that appeared in 1987.

***

The film's storyline was simple. It begins in spring 1939. An Eighth Route Army soldier tasked with collecting folk songs for the army's propaganda work travels on foot around the bleak landscape of northern Shaanxi, when he comes across a small family living on the edge of poverty: the father, a widower older than his years; his fourteen-year-old daughter; and her younger brother. The daughter, destined to be married to a much older man in a few months, pleads with the soldier to take her away with him, but his duties make it impossible. When he goes back to the CCP's Yan'an headquarters, the soldier witnesses the vigor and revolutionary spirit shown by normally taciturn peasants. Meanwhile, shrinking from the embrace of her new husband, the girl resolves to flee to Yan'an but in crossing the Yellow River is engulfed in its waves. When the soldier returns to the village during the summer, he sees the village men are taking part in a prayer ceremony for rain, showing the same vigor as their Yan'an counterparts. The film alternates between passages of stillness, accentuating the vastness of the arid landscape, and extraordinarily vigorous religious and social ceremonies. A large part of the film's success is due to this alternation, made even more emphatic by the contrast between the strident colors of festive events against the bleakly yellow landscape.

In the five years that followed the film's release in Beijing on August 19, 1984, *The Yellow Earth* became famous beyond anyone's expectations, not only for the extraordinary impact it was making in China, from film critics to audiences and then more generally to academic and literary commentators but also for the huge, enthusiastic audiences it attracted, especially in Hong Kong. When the film was released abroad, its reception was just as enthusiastic; the only country in which it failed to appeal was Poland, whose audiences saw it as just another effort in socialist realism. In response to this international excitement, I decided to supplement the script with a substantial account of its origins, meanings, and reception. The final version of the book includes a preface; shots from the film and of the director in action; and ten chapters covering the film's plot, production process, release, and public debates about it in China and abroad, as well as the director's personal history. It concludes with a glossary followed by the script. It took me a rather long time to learn how to translate the technical vocabulary and conventions of film scripts; in the end, the translation itself was a bare eighty-eight pages. If it seems as if the script was of secondary importance, it wouldn't be particularly surprising to me: like the literary version, a script alone cannot convey the power of the film itself. To be frank, the translation is not an easy or exciting read. The merit of the film is both conceptual and visual; it has little to do with written literature, and its political stance was and remains open to more than a single interpretation.

As I completed these chapters in 1985, I approached *Renditions* about book publication. John Minford was enthusiastic and helped a lot in planning the book's format over the next couple of years, but when I finally submitted the complete manuscript to *Renditions* in 1987, the new editor suggested that the book was more academic research than translation. It was then suggested in 1988 that the commentary chapters should be relegated to separate publication somewhere as an article, and in 1989 I was informed that my manuscript would not be published by *Renditions*. The British Film Institute had already also replied to my inquiries saying that "we cannot consider publishing a book on such a young director who has only made two films." Faber & Faber was more welcoming, offering in 1988 to publish both *The Yellow Earth* and *King* of the Children (*Haizi Wang* 孩子王, another of Chen Kaige's work); the only problem was that they wouldn't be able to do these projects for a year. In connection with Faber & Faber's offer, I wrote to John Minford in March 1988 about the complicated issues relating to royalties:

> Normally I try to be overgenerous with the authors I translate and ask for a 70:30 division of royalties in favor of the author. But who is the author of the film script YE [*The Yellow Earth*]? I know for a fact that Kaige did a hell of a lot of work on it, and it seems grossly unfair if he should be excluded from the royalties. (They may even amount to something substantial.) Also, if F&F only want my translation and not the extra bits written by me, I'll still only ask for 70:30, but if they also want my work as well then I think it should be upped to 60:40. What do you think?
>
> It's a different problem with HZW [*Haizi wang: King of the Children*]. I did the subtitles and of course I would use them as the basis for the film script (though of course not necessarily identical). But I have never been paid for the subtitles, and in fact I don't even know if they are being used, if they've been used but with alternation, credited or not credited etc. Also, should the "authors" also include Ah Cheng? The script is credited to Chen Maiping and Chen Kaige: would that be enough?

John Minford responded with a telegram to the effect that because the *Renditions* negotiations would only start in late 1989, he would advise me to go ahead with Faber & Faber, with possible reserved rights for *Renditions* in Hong Kong and the US. In the end, it was T. L. Tsim, the director of The Chinese University Press, whose enthusiasm led to a happy conclusion in 1991, when the press published my manuscript. I have only praise for T. L. Tsim, who has all along been one of my most helpful and supportive publishers, and The Chinese University Press for keeping me informed throughout the whole period the book was in print.

Spoken and Unspoken Words

***

In January 1985, Chen Kaige had given me power of attorney to represent his "professional interests in regard to all film, literary and publishing activities." This appointment quietly expired without anything much having been achieved. I was still in Beijing, teaching translation at the college and living on campus, when Chen Kaige decided to recruit me for a voiceover in his second film *The Grand Parade* (*Da yuebing* 大阅兵). I was asked to draft some lines in a scene where one of the soldiers is learning English. At that time, learning English seemed to be one of the country's most popular activities, so the idea was that the soldier was a young man with ambitions to improve himself by listening to English lessons on the radio. I still have a copy of the truly amateurish dialogue, jointly constructed by the two of us, that Chen Kaige recorded in my small flat. This episode was deleted from the final version, although unhappily this improvement was not enough to save the film. Clumsily translated as *The Big Parade* and released in 1986, the film was mainly notable for its lack of success. Another director would have retreated; Chen Kaige instead became even more ambitious.

In December 1985 Chen Kaige's father, previously a member of the Nationalist Party (Guomindang), was admitted to the Chinese Communist Party. Chen Kaige made a speech for the event. According to his sister, however, Chen Kaige was at that time often in a black mood. In those years, he experienced a great deal of conflict both at home with his parents and within himself.[3] Taking advantage of his dazzling new fame, he was planning to accept the large volume of invitations to film festivals or speaking tours, but the authorities were still cagey about letting him accept all of these invitations.

***

In January 1986 I moved to Oslo and was impressed immediately with the generosity of travel grants in academic life. In September that year, for instance, I paid a short visit to Beijing, the highlight of which was seeing

Chen Kaige playing the role of the Captain of the Guard in Bernardo Bertolucci's *The Last Emperor*. Chen Kaige hadn't ridden a horse before, and his English still wasn't easy to understand, but both drawbacks were handsomely overcome by his impressive physique and confidence. After his performance in this movie, he set out for southwest China and the following month formally sent me a letter of invitation to visit Mengla, a rural village chosen for the site of his new film.

Chen Kaige's third film *King of the Children*, released in 1987, restored to a large extent his reputation as one of China's most original directors among Chinese audiences and sinologists. As noted later, however, non-Chinese viewers were not impressed, possibly because of its poor subtitles. Meanwhile, the script was undergoing the many changes required by the Xi'an Film Studio, for which Chen Maiping, under his pen name Wan Zhi, drafted a series of revised scripts. The film is based on a story by Ah Cheng, a writer whom the director personally knew well and admired but who was then living in the US; for this and possibly for other reasons, Ah Cheng was not asked for assistance at any point in the filming.

After visiting several other sites in southwest China, Chen Kaige had settled on a small village in subtropical Xishuangbanna, in Yunnan, along China's border with Myanmar and Laos: the scenery was lush, the mountains high, the population only partly dominated by the Han people. It was also the area where both he and Ah Cheng had spent several years working on rubber plantations during the Cultural Revolution.[4] In Chen Kaige's case, this was followed by a spell in a local army unit, to which he'd been recruited largely for his height and bulk, which also helped in winning local basketball tournaments. He also took part in cross-border forays with the Viet Cong.[5] Although the Cultural Revolution had subsided almost a decade earlier, he was still constantly being reminded of those years in these remote, economically deprived areas. Chen Kaige was reliving youthful memories, some of them bracing, most of them still bitter.

Spoken and Unspoken Words

***

In December 1986, I made the long journey from Oslo to Beijing and thence to Xishuangbanna. I'd been provided with a mimeograph of the film script dated September 1986 (a few months before the actual filming took place). The main heading described it as the film's *juben* 剧本, a term that usually indicated a literary script. Below the film's name was a line to the effect that it was the director's working *taiben*. Chen Kaige signed his name below that for me.

When I arrived in Jinghong, the prefectural seat of the Xishuangbanna Dai Autonomous Prefecture, the police first refused to allow me to travel to the countryside where the film was being shot. When I managed to convince them that I was not in the business of illegally smuggling rare native plants out of China (the term *biaoben* 标本, referring to native plant specimens, left me staring blankly at them), I was allowed to proceed. After an overnight stay at the local hotel where the friendly staff invited me to share their dinner, I was conveyed the next morning by a creaky old bus to the nearest township. On the way there, the bus stopped at a small village. A local woman carrying a baby in her arms with a toddler by her side approached me and offered to sell me the baby, a girl, for the ring I was wearing. It was a cheap fake silver ring that I'd purchased at the Beijing Hotel. I could only decline.

At the final stop, I transferred to a hired car that took me from Mengla village to the Tropical Botany Guesthouse, a modest building housing the film crew. There was no shooting that day because they had run out of film two days earlier, but Chen Kaige was at work in his separate suite, a two-room apartment. It had a bedroom with a double bed that had a pink bedspread and a pink mosquito net, and another room that contained a cupboard piled high with papers, a small table covered with bottled and tinned foodstuffs, another small table used for meals, and a large desk, also covered with papers. On the desk was a table lamp in the shape of a piano which lit up when you lifted the lid, but it stopped working the day after I arrived, and no one bothered to fix it. This room served Chen Kaige as a living room, dining room, office, meeting room, and rehearsal studio. Gu Changwei, the cinematographer, had a room next door, and they shared a bathroom, but the Western-style plumbing was broken, and there was no water for the bathtub as far as I could see. Instead, there were large plastic buckets of water for washing.

The rest of the film crew, whom I joined, were housed in the main building, with shared bedrooms that frequently had no electricity or running water. The occupants usually had candles in the rooms, and most of them had flashlights; these were necessary for going to the lavatory at night. The common lavatory was located a five-to-ten-minute walk toward the fields. It was cleaned once a day and usually wasn't too awful. Many of the men didn't bother to use the lavatory at night but used the bushes around the dormitory guesthouse.

***

The day after I arrived, we set out before dawn on another creaky old bus for a scene where the schoolchildren were to assemble before tramping up the mountainside to cut bamboo. We reached the site at about 6:30 a.m., but the mist had already disappeared. We still had to wait for the schoolchildren, who were the main actors in this scene, to arrive, and then we all trooped down to the gully for the morning's action. First, some bushes had to be hacked away; next, the stream proved to be too noisy. As the crew tried to dam the stream and set up artificial smoke, it struck me how much they had to interfere with nature to make this film. As the setup was being constructed, I passed the time chatting to the crew who were not actively engaged; I also tried to relieve the alternatively boring and tense shooting by teaching them the part-song "Row, row, row your boat, / Gently down the stream, / Merrily, merrily, merrily, / Life is but a dream," settling on two rather than four parts. The words were easily translatable into Chinese. Two years later, I noticed that the Educated Youth in "The King of Trees" (released the year before my visit to Xishuangbanna) sing a part-song that sounds very close to this.[6]

Spoken and Unspoken Words

Accompanying the film crew was a representative from the local forestry protection unit, but neither he nor anyone else seemed to care about the discarded smoke canisters, litter, or attempts to manipulate the scenery. The only time there was a problem was when the children, bored with waiting, started hacking at a tree trunk across the stream: the alarm was not because they were destroying the tree but that they were disfiguring it for the camera. On my first day, I asked why these scenes were always shot from behind: Chen Kaige explained that the main purpose of these scenes was the scenery itself. The following day, a bench was placed behind him for me so that I could see what was happening, but Chen Kaige drily pointed out that shooting was only a start, and I could learn more about the film when it was being cut later in Beijing.

I'd brought with me a copy of a groundbreaking anthology on contemporary Chinese literature, edited by Geremie Barmé and John Minford. Called *Seeds of Fire: Chinese Voices of Conscience*, it had appeared a few months earlier in a prescient response to the first signs of encroaching crisis then beginning to appear in China. Published by *The Far Eastern Economic Review*, it had attracted a large and fearful audience.[7] The crew, including Chen Kaige, was pleased to see that it contained passages from *The Yellow Earth*, and a lively discussion on current debates on contemporary literature followed. I was dismayed, however, by the attribution of the synopsis of *The Yellow Earth* to actor and writer Zhang Ziliang. It was by me. John later made a satisfying apology.

***

At the start, I saw little of Chen Kaige, who would spend the better part of each day with actual filming and most evenings revising the script under pressure from the political supervisor (who probably should be regarded as the script's coauthor). Later, perhaps when the pressure diminished as the shooting went ahead, he was more present. He explained that the basic message of the film was to undermine the prevalence of copying in Chinese culture. He was very strict with the crew, most of whom were supplied by the film studio (he'd only been allowed to choose his main colleagues). At one point, he summoned the whole crew and explained why he was so strict while thanking them for their cooperation. He specifically mentioned in this general assembly that some crew members had made some excellent suggestions (this was another indication that Ah Cheng's script was far from being followed in all respects). Nevertheless, Chen Kaige made no gestures toward running a calm, cooperative outfit: when he was angry, he showed it. (I once got in the way of shooting and was castigated for it.)

Filming on location lasted for about a week. I then spent a week with the film crew traveling from Xishuangbanna to Kunming and from there to Xi'an for the editing process, including the sound editing. There I carried out further interviews with the film crew and had discussions with representatives of the Xi'an Film Studio about the production and distribution of the film. We finally straggled to Beijing for the music soundtrack and other technical editing, a final screening, and a two-day seminar on the film. As the first rushes of the film were being developed, I was able to see drafts of the scenes I had seen shot as well as earlier scenes. I discussed with the director and cinematographer their ideas on editing these rushes. I also interviewed the director's family and others in the film world on the current state of filmmaking and the cinema in China and gathered much valuable information.

During this time, my suggestion for the English translation of the film's title was adopted, and after the director checked them, I submitted a set of English subtitles in time for the film's release. Celebrations were held when the film board announced that the film was passed for release, and again when it won favorable reviews in the Chinese media and was selected for the Cannes Film Festival to be held in May 1988.

According to the report I made to the Norwegian government at the end of March 1987, I was able to watch every scene shot during the week I spent in Xishuangbanna and was present at rehearsals and meetings discussing the next day's work. I took notes on the film's direction,

Spoken and Unspoken Words 119

cinematography, acting, set design, costuming, makeup, lighting, and sound. Of special interest were the departures from the script which took place during shooting, rehearsals, and meetings. I interviewed each of the chief crew members and most of their assistants on their previous work experience, recruitment for this film, experiences with this film, and professional opinions on the Chinese cinema. Some photographs from this visit appear in *The Yellow Earth* book.

***

Translating a film script, or, even worse, subtitling it, is not much fun for me because dialogue is my weak point and usually requires declamation rather than subtlety. However, after I'd become involved in the film I decided that I could cope. Chen Kaige had already suggested in 1986 that I should translate the film script of *King of the Children,* and later it was agreed I would also translate the Chinese subtitles as they appeared to the version of the film privately screened at the Beijing Film Studio in August 1987. Around this time my health was becoming a cause for concern; juggling translation publications involving Bei Dao, Chen Maiping, and Chen Kaige was also becoming a problem. Then in September 1988, I discovered that the English subtitles to the film then being shown in Britain and America were provided by the Chinese Film Export Import Corporation.

Like other subtitles provided by the corporation, this set had serious shortcomings that were mostly due either to carelessness or to an inadequate understanding of English. For example, a mildly obscene expression is deleted in a scene when the teacher (the "king," a young lad who'd barely graduated from primary school) is being teased, although elsewhere other obscenities are retained; this deletion makes nonsense of the surrounding dialogue. In another scene, where the teacher is explaining how to write the character for the word "life," the whole dialogue has been deleted, and the scene becomes unintelligible to the English-language viewer.

The most insensitive case of mistranslation occurs in the scene where the children read out their compositions, which of course are all ungrammatical. In the corporation's version, however, the village children's compositions are corrected, thereby destroying a significant message about what the children have (and haven't) learned from their teacher, and again the surrounding dialogue becomes meaningless. Misspellings and typographical errors are also rife: for example, the word "loose" is repeatedly given as "lose."

My translation of the song sung by children at the end of the film, however, was adopted (apart from two or three words) by the corporation without acknowledgement (perhaps it was regarded as too trivial). I'd gone to some effort to provide rhymes, so it was clear that the translation was indisputably mine, but no acknowledgement or payment has ever been made to me. It also follows that the corporation possessed a copy of my subtitles but (with this small exception) chose not to use them.

***

A report on the film's reception at Cannes in 1988 appeared in the London newspaper *The Independent*, which ran a story in its arts section on the film's reception at Cannes, claiming that the *China Daily* had reported that the film was given "the Golden Alarm Clock Award for the most boring film." This "news" was due to a misunderstanding: some journalists in Cannes had suggested the "award" as a joke. It was not a good beginning. Further reviews were lukewarm (possibly because its English subtitles were so poor), and in some countries new sets of subtitles were attached. Whatever the reason, overseas viewers unfamiliar with Chinese were not impressed, and the reception outside China never achieved the international fame enjoyed by Chen Kaige's *The Yellow Earth* or or his later 1993 film *Farewell My Concubine*.

Translating poetry and film are so very different: it would be highly unusual, for instance, for a translator to be standing next to someone composing a poem and to be commenting on the process. It is rare enough

Spoken and Unspoken Words

for the translator to be passed on a handwritten poem from the author shortly after its completion. A film script, particularly in China where politics are all-important, is not the creation of a single individual but a work that passes through many hands before location shooting and again during editing. Nevertheless, I witnessed in Xishuangbanna how the script, even after being approved by the relevant authorities during and after its completion and being exposed to audiences and their opinions worldwide, could still be a director's massively personal statement.

***

In June 1988, I was delighted to receive an invitation from Faber & Faber to submit my translation of the film script for book publication along with other material about the film. I was not provided with any other information about the book's appearance or contents before it appeared in 1989. The first sign that this publication might be imperfect was the front cover, where the title is given as *King of the Children & the New Chinese Cinema*. A correct version only appears on the title page, which reads: *King of the Children* [by] Chen Kaige and Wan Zhi and *The New Chinese Cinema / an Introduction* [by] Tony Rayns. The problems continue with the placement of the definite article. The difference between "the king of children" (my choice) and "king of the children" is this: "the king of children" is not a child, whereas a "king of the children" is. I don't know if any distinction was discussed by the book's editors, but this grated on me. Although the use of "the" in "King of the Children" counts as mistranslation, at least it sounds like English. The problem is that the title doesn't match the narrative, the "king" himself not being one of the children. There's not much difference in age or learning between the teacher and the children, however, so the use of the definite article would not give a blatantly false impression to the reader.

But there are also a large number of errors that occur throughout the book, including changes made without any consultation with me about my own contributions, and information attributed to others which originated from me. Even worse, material from my translation was incorporated in the editor's introduction, implying that it was the editor's own conclusion; and if that weren't insulting enough, much of the information supplied in the introduction and the footnotes to my translation (added without my knowledge or consent) is incorrect.

One of these many instances was so egregious that it remains a vivid scar in my memory. An absurd double error is the statement in the footnotes is that the Chinese word *zhiqing* means "educated youth" and that it's untranslatable. It doesn't, and it isn't. I've always been opposed to the practice of non-translation, when the translator chooses not to translate special terms in the original language. In particular, it had been my consistent practice in both editions of my translations of Ah Cheng's work to translate *zhiqing*, an abbreviation of *zhishi qingnian* (meaning educated youth) as EY (plural: EYs).[8] The abbreviation was so common in China at that time that the author of the film script that I used didn't bother to use the full expression, but I felt it was useful for the translation to introduce it on first mention. There is no indication, however, in the Faber & Faber introduction, that the term is an abbreviation that has become thoroughly familiarized in conversation. The suggestion in the introduction that the non-translation was my choice and that the expression "resists translation" is wholly incorrect.

A similar error is the claim that the term "king of children" is "an obsolete word for teacher": it isn't used in formal discourse these days, but it's certainly not obsolete. One up-to-date example is its use in the name of a rock band in Kaohsiung (a large city in southern Taiwan), which started in 2012 and still active as least as recently in 2018.[9] I still see no duty to impose an ugly, unpronounceable, and meaningless romanization when a perfectly good translation is available.

It's generally been accepted by literary translators that although personal names and surnames are mostly better not translated, nicknames or pen names are usually translated because they hint at the person's character. In the original story, the teacher appears just once under his nickname, Lao Gan 老干. The word *lao*, meaning "old" is a common prefix for informal address among males of all ages; the word *gan* is explained by the young man as indicating that he was skinny (or possibly underfed). After many trials, I'd hit on "Beanpole" as the English equivalent. This nickname, however, inexplicably appears in the Faber & Faber version as "Lao Gar," using the "r" suffix common in informal discourse in north China. But "*gar*" does not occur in any form in the original Chinese text of either the story or the film script. Even more baffling is the claim in the introduction "that 'Beanpole' might be the nearest equivalent," as if that translation were invented in the course of writing the introduction. It wasn't.

I was also taken aback by the lack of reference to Ah Cheng, the original author of the novella "The King of Children," who is mentioned only twice throughout the whole book and briefly at that.[10] Further, there is no mention on the cover, the title page, or the list of contents that I was the translator and editor of *King of the Children*'s script, although I'd provided the translator's note, the director's note, the cast list, and finally the script's translation, altogether making up more than half of the book. Also not mentioned anywhere in the book itself is that parts of my translation were rewritten without any prior consultation with me and in a manner I did not approve.

***

One error in judgement for which the publisher (rather than the editor) should be held responsible is the suppression of the translator's name on the book's cover, if only, in this particular instance, because there is more translation in the book than any other material. But in general, writers, editors, publishers, distributors, booksellers, and readers rarely question what should appear on a cover and whose name should appear on the title page. Most people take for granted that the author will be on the cover; this much is obvious. (Modest authors may use pseudonyms.) Is it less commonly agreed that the translator's name should also appear on the dust jacket, book cover, or title page? I'm biased, of course, but it seems to me that if readers and publishers want translations that are both conscientious and imaginative, for heaven's sake give translators credit for what they do.

I appreciate that some readers look for the thrill of the exotic, but it's not a reaction that I aim for as a translator; there is enough exotic flavor in geographical names or personal names and surnames. If personal names are translated, it may be argued, they appear even more exotic. However, a surfeit of exotica can also be tiresome. Place names and measurements raise similar problems, and most translators probably have their own preferences, but editorial staff have no business changing them without consulting (or, at a minimum, informing) the translators. It would have been so simple, had I been given a chance to see the proofs, for me to have corrected not only the many errors introduced into my translation but those in the rest of the book as well.

It may seem ridiculous to go to such lengths in picking over someone's errors as I've done here: my excuse is to draw your attention, dear reader, to how attached translators become to their work and how insulted we feel when it is rejected, rephrased, or otherwise clumsily edited. I wrote a long letter to the editor when I first received a copy in September 1989 and received apologies later the same month, when an undertaking was made to correct the errors and omissions should there be a reprint. In his apology, the editor also confessed to being unaware of the stipulation in my contract that the translator's name should be on the cover or the title page. At the same time, I received a four-page letter from the author of the introduction, complaining of my "catalogue of venom and abuse."

In October the editor wrote to confirm a list of amendments to be made in any new edition, including an assurance that I was to be given notice of any such edition and that final proofs of that edition would be sent to me. As far as I am aware, no reprint or new edition ever appeared. Shortly after this correspondence, I disowned the "translation" as it presently stands and will also continue to make public my distance

Spoken and Unspoken Words 125

from the book. The book itself was declared out of print and remaindered in a statement dated June 1999; the last statement I received is dated March 2003, showing a still unearned balance of £173.32. To be fair, the book in other respects is worth a (cautious) look. I've noted only one typo: "fface" on page 91.

***

In July 1988 I had an interview with Chen Kaige in New York, but we did not discuss the Faber & Faber fiasco. Fortunately, my book *The Yellow Earth: A Film by Chen Kaige* was published by The Chinese University Press in Hong Kong in 1991. It was a bestseller for several years but is now out of print.

Although my book on *The Yellow Earth* proved successful, I never solved to my satisfaction the problem of translating film, a process distant from translating written literature. Among other difficulties, the film translator ideally needs to see the development of the film as it's being shot. Moreover, because much of any film depends on its visual and aural impact, it seems impossible that the translation of the script can ever do it justice. Adding to this is an additional burden that is imposed by the organization of a film crew: the director's apparently autocratic position may be at least in part illusionary, and the script is just a guide. I'm still not sure to which the translator should defer.

In any case, it marked the virtual end of my engagement with contemporary mainland writing. With the exception of Ah Cheng the only such writing I've translated since then are works by two women: a novella and a short story, both commissioned.[11] Instead, after moving to Norway in 1986, I focused on Chinese authors living outside of China; then, moving on to Edinburgh in 1990, I became immersed in Lu Xun and Xu Guangping's love letters.

***

Many years later, I've begun to think in terms of a new formula: "I own my own words," easily convertible to "you own your own words" and "we own our own words."

Notes

1. See entries on Ding Xilin's six short plays in *The Drama*, edited by Bernd Eberstein, vol. 4, *A Selective Guide to Chinese Literature 1900–1949* (Leiden: Brill, 1990), 97–106.
2. Chen Kaige, "The Masked Dance," trans. Bonnie McDougall, 219–227.
3. He told me this in our personal communications.
4. For more on their years in southwest China see chapter 11.
5. His Viet Cong experience is mentioned in an interview published in the *International Herald Tribune*, May 22–23, 1993, 9.
6. Ah Cheng, *Three Kings,* 104, 10.
7. Three years later, months after the June Fourth massacres of 1989, a new expanded edition under the same title came out.
8. I have used capital letters for this expression in order to signify that it's part of a slogan and not an ordinary descriptive term.
9. They call themselves Kid King, and sing in Taiwanese; see <https://zh.wikipedia.org/wiki/haiziwang 孩子王_(樂團)>; thanks to Anders Hansson for this information.
10. My translation of the title of this story has always been "The King of Children." It was published as such, together with "The King of Chess" and "The King of Trees," in the London and New York versions of Ah Cheng's novellas. These books were entitled *Three Kings* and *The King of Trees* respectively. It became *King of the Children* in the Faber & Faber version (about Chen Kaige's film).
11. See, for example, works by Wang Anyi and Tie Ning discussed in chapters 11 and 13.

CHAPTER 9

SHADOWS IN EXILE

In January 1986, I took a plane from Beijing to Oslo, where I would remain for four years. My husband and son had already left, making the same journey by train. Bei Dao, Chen Maiping, and Chen Kaige came to the airport to see me off. It had been an extraordinary five years in my life, both personally and professionally. Leaving China meant that I was also leaving opportunities for an intimate understanding of contemporary writing there. I would no longer encounter new translations such as those that had been taking up most of my time. Instead, I would spend the next two decades recirculating the translations I had already done.

With Bei Dao's poetry reaching international audiences, it was time to publish an enhanced selection from the now substantial pile of manuscripts still building up in Beijing. In Oslo, after having carefully nursed the augmented pile on the plane, I put together *The August Sleepwalker*, which was published by Anvil Press Poetry in London in 1988; Bei Dao became the first PRC writer whose poetry and fiction in English translation were published by a major British publisher.[1] As in *Notes from the City of the Sun*, my name appears on the cover and title page, and both Bei Dao and I received royalties. I also chose the title; some years later, it was derided by an English colleague by being pronounced with the accent on the second syllable of "August," that is, playing with the difference between "August" (the month) and "august" (meaning respected and impressive).

Peter Jay, the owner of Anvil Press Poetry, was also its chief editor, and the most helpful and dedicated editor I've had the good fortune to know. I owe a great deal to his dedication to supporting poetry and poetry translation and remain grateful for his advice, especially for where and how to trim wordiness or excessive poeticism. It was sad to hear from him in 2015 that he'd decided to close Anvil Press. The copyright for *The August Sleepwalker* along with responsibility for royalties has since been transferred to northern England–based Carcanet Press, Britain's leading publisher specializing in poetry. A revised version of *The August Sleepwalker* was also published by New Directions in New York in 1990. Bei Dao and I continue to receive a small set of royalties from Carcanet Press not so much from book sales as for unspecified rights (presumably republication of some of the poems).

A brief note on the verso page of *The August Sleepwalker* explains where some of these poems had been previously published: forty-one from *Notes of the City of Sun* are included, along with an additional fifty. The poems are not dated but are divided into three sections, also undated but known to be 1970–1978, 1979–1983, and 1983–1986. The main contents are preceded by my five-page introduction and short translator's note. The title poem heads the final section: it is uncharacteristically optimistic in tone, suggesting that the turmoil in China in the Cultural Revolution might be replaced by a more humane social and political structure. I'm still glad it's there, although, starting 1986–1987, China's history would become even more violent. The following commentary, adapted from the introduction, retains its subdued optimism.

***

Bei Dao was educated at one of the country's top schools, attended by the offspring of China's ruling elite, and in the normal course of events would presumably have taken his place as a loyal beneficiary of the system. Instead, the Cultural Revolution destroyed expectations of cooperation between the CCP and intellectual elites. Like many of the offspring of now disgraced urban families, Bei Dao became a member of the vigorous new Red Guards movement. Eventually disillusioned by the movement's own violence and factionalism, however, Bei Dao abandoned direct political action. Thereafter, he became an outsider, asserting his individual position through poetry and fiction.

Bei Dao and his fellow underground poets of the early 1970s were creating an alternative Chinese literature: in language, imagery, syntax, and structure, their poetry is highly original and obviously experimental. The subjective, intimate voice in Bei Dao's love poetry had not been heard in China for three decades; even more significant was the poet's plunge into the irrational, in what was not only a defiant act of moral courage but also an act of faith in poetry's function to reveal or discover fundamental truths of human existence. Bei Dao's early poetry is a revelation of two unreal universes: a dream world of love and tranquility that should exist but does not, and a nightmare of cruelty, terror, and hatred that should not exist but does.

Such poetry was to the authorities of the time an unforgivable act of defiance. Bei Dao's most famous poem, "The Answer," written in spring 1976, was a clear challenge to the discredited political leadership, marking his emergence from underground to dissident in the unofficial literary movement of 1978–1979. In the reform years that followed, new writers like Bei Dao were drawn into the new cultural bureaucracy and published their work in the national press. From the mid-1980s, however, a new wave of disillusionment spread among the former activists: Bei Dao's work became characterized by a colder, clinical language, and its imagery became more impenetrable while its emotional force grew keener. Only in a remote, private corner are there still moments of tenderness and tranquility, with passages of love, affection, and trust.

Bei Dao's poetry is not fundamentally an act of political engagement with the system but a statement of personal concerns that can only be contained by distancing it in writing. Its so-called obscurity is not simply adopted for reasons of expedience but is an emotional necessity for the preservation of rationality. It is not blind sympathy with all suffering: it is respect for basic human needs and desires as well as an affirmation of the sanctity of the individual's private world. The peculiar tension between the density and transparency of the poems is an echo of the poet's dual commitment to revelation and communication. Few of Bei Dao's poems can be called happy. The most positive emotions are an appreciation of the healing powers of nature, love, and companionship, together with a kind of cheerfulness in the face of adversity. Bei Dao's search for the self holds universal meaning. His devotion to art is not a temporary escape from society or politics but a commitment to nonpolitical communication.

It is fair to claim that Bei Dao's poetry is translatable because its most striking features are powerful imagery and significant structure. The images are mostly derived from natural and urban phenomena as familiar to readers outside China as within, not particularized as specific names of places, people, or local commodities. The structure of the poems is similarly based on universal geometrical or logical patterns, and the language does not rely heavily on a particular vocabulary or special musical effects. The surface texture of the poems is therefore not significantly affected by translation into English (I can't comment on other languages). Beyond this semantic level are the poems' basic concerns. Although directly inspired by immediate problems in the author's own life and environment, they look to the core of the problems and not their outward trappings. Their interest to foreign readers does not lie primarily in the political role they have sometimes assumed in contemporary China but in their grasp of human dilemmas present in varying degrees in all modern societies.

The reaction to the publication of this translation was overwhelming: one of the most encouraging was its selection as one of the best books of the year in the 1985 annual review in the *Times Literary Supplement*. I have also witnessed responses at many readings over the years in Chinese, English, or both, to enraptured audiences in Europe and Hong Kong. The most memorable occasion was a reading in Hong Kong in 2006, for which the translation department at CUHK had booked one of the largest halls on campus (it still ended up with standing room only). Bei Dao read a poem in Chinese followed by me reciting the English translation, while both versions appeared on the screen behind us. The reading finished with a warm embrace between the two of us (it had been a long time since we'd last met). The audience went wild with applause. At another reading some years later at the City University of Hong Kong, this time in Chinese only, the reception was just as enthusiastic, and the sight of the long stream of students queueing up to have their copies signed was inspiring.

***

I'd sought help from several Chinese informants in translating Bei Dao's poems, as consulting his colleagues instead of the author seemed less awkward. The most prominent of these helpers was Chen Maiping, who had been the fiction editor of *Jintian* as well as the author of several short stories that first appeared there. The first to be published in translation was "Open Ground" (*Kaikuodi* 开阔地), then his most famous story, printed in the *Bulletin of Concerned Asian Scholars* in 1984 and reprinted in *Contemporary Chinese Literature* in 1985; I'm listed as sole translator but sought assistance from the author.[2] Other stories were co-translated with Kam Louie, my colleague in Sydney: one was printed in *Renditions* 26 in 1986 and a selection of three more appeared in *Renditions* 52 in 1999. Chen Maiping left China in 1986 for Norway and then moved to Sweden, where he still lives.

Not everyone has agreed with my translation. One young critic, for example, claimed that the word "beloved" was "archaic," a revelation that came as quite a surprise. Otherwise, the reviews have been favorable, and

The August Sleepwalker has itself been translated into several languages. Most welcome have been innumerable requests to include the poems in anthologies of all kinds for a wide variety of readers. Of all my translations over a period of some fifty years, *The August Sleepwalker* garnered the widest circulation outside China.

***

Bei Dao's next collection in English was *Old Snow*; Chen Maiping was my co-translator, and most of the translation was carried out when we were both living in Oslo. During this time, Bei Dao was often traveling, mainly in the US and Europe. In 1988 he spent several months in Durham as a guest of the Durham University, this time accompanied by his wife and child. I made a brief trip to Durham to meet them, although Bei Dao soon took off again, leaving Shao Fei and their daughter, Tiantian, in the hands of Durham locals; they were mainly left alone.

The poems in *Old Snow* show the influence on Bei Dao's poetry of Scandinavian writers and their audiences. We'd introduced Bei Dao to sinologists at the Swedish embassy in Beijing in the early 1980s as well as to Göran Malmqvist, who was a member of the selection board for the Nobel Prize for Literature. Malmqvist soon translated poems by Bei Dao and the younger poet Gu Cheng for a single volume that was well received in Sweden. In 1985, Bei Dao received permission to travel abroad, so it seemed like a good idea to introduce Bei Dao to Swedish poetry, so I obtained for him a copy of *Modern Scandinavian Poetry 1900–1975* (1982). Because his English was still imperfect, I selected a batch of Swedish poems and explained their meaning and structure; Danish and Norwegian friends performed a similar service, but it was the Swedish material that occupied Bei Dao's attention, in particular, the four poems by Tomas Tranströmer. A few years later, Bei Dao was finally able to accept the many invitations he had received from Sweden (where he had the pleasure of meeting Tranströmer) and other countries, and as his fame grew his poetry was translated into more and more languages.

He also gave readings, talks, and interviews, enhancing his reputation as one of China's most talented writers.

***

Anders had purchased our first computer, a Macintosh 128K, in 1985. At first it was nothing but a foreign object on which I was able to make a fair copy for printing, and it took me a year or two to abandon any other form of scripting. After I left Beijing in early 1986 for the University of Oslo, I was also provided with a Macintosh Plus (soon upgraded to a Macintosh SE) at my university office, and all of us by now had begun to believe we needed to use computers (a decade or so later computing launched our son on his professional career). For me, the ease of writing, revision, and experimentation was a huge advance, opening the way for greater productivity when I resumed active translation. It took me much longer to recognize the second main benefit of new technology: the ability to dispense with most footnotes both in translation and research publications, on the assumption that readers could look up allusions by using their search engines.

Absence from Beijing brought other unexpected benefits, including a lively correspondence with lots of local gossip from Gladys Yang. I remember telling her about a young Englishman trying to pretend he represented Bei Dao in regard to Heinemann's reprint of The Chinese University Press's publication of *Waves*. Not surprisingly, Bei Dao had become a valuable "commodity."

Chen Maiping had arrived in Oslo in 1987, bolstering our translations of Bei Dao's new output; our next set began to appear in various journals, including *Grand Street*, *Manhattan Review*, and *New Directions 54*. Soon there was enough for a new collection. In June the same year, I received an invitation to attend a reception in honor of the thirty-fifth anniversary of the FLP's foundation but was obliged to decline. Later, "The Clock" (*Zimingzhong xia* 自鸣钟下) by Wan Zhi (Chen Maiping), co-translated with Kam Louie, was published in *Renditions* in 1987.[3]

Unfortunately, my previously excellent relations with *Renditions* were coming under some pressure. My private (as well as professional) life was also getting complicated: in 1988, I was told an eye infection was leading to blindness; fortunately, after nearly a year, this diagnosis proved to be false.

***

In 1988 I'd received a major research grant to bring Chinese writers and artists to the University of Oslo, which included a visit from Bei Dao for six months from September 1989 to March 1990. The nature of his activities had been left open. Bei Dao had left Beijing in April 1989 to take up a four-month grant in Berlin; invitations to go from there to Aarhus in Denmark and then on to Oslo with his wife and daughter had also been arranged. When news of the June Fourth demonstrations and their violent suppression reached Europe, Bei Dao's hosts adjusted his schedule so that his arrival in Oslo was put forward by several months. Bei Dao arrived in Oslo as planned, but his family was unable to join him.

In response to these new circumstances, I proposed that Bei Dao's contribution to the Oslo research grant program would be relaunching *Jintian*, and to make this possible I provided the cash to buy a computer for use by Bei Dao and Chen Maiping. Bei Dao had raised the idea of a relaunch early in 1988 but had been dissuaded; now he was unsure whether it could attract a sufficient number of contributors and readers. It was ultimately decided to invite up to a dozen Chinese writers now living abroad to come to Oslo to decide whether and how to proceed. This assembly took place in April 1990. Those present included Xu Xing, Duo Duo, Yang Lian, Liu Suola, Gao Xingjian, and Zha Jianying, in addition to Bei Dao and Chen Maiping.

It was obvious to me that the assembly should make its decisions on these vital matters in private, although under pressure it was finally agreed that a final session would be open to Chinese students in Oslo and to a handful of European sinologists. It was also arranged that a further session open to the public would be held in Stockholm, together with an invitation to Bei Dao to spend some time in Stockholm after his stay in Oslo. At the initial session in Oslo, it was agreed that the relaunch would go ahead with Bei Dao as the head of a *Jintian* editorial board and Chen Maiping as editor in chief. In addition, The Today Foundation with Bei Dao as its head was set up to secure funding from international foundations. Many well-known Chinese and Western writers and sinologists subsequently accepted invitations to join the Today Foundation. A comprehensive account of these events was published by Chen Maiping in the centenary edition of *Jintian*, quoting Li Yu's poem on the frailty of human coexistence:

> Gathered, they scattered; the divided now join,
> All become rivers in stream and blossoms in fall.[4]

Following the June Fourth massacres, a new expanded edition of the groundbreaking anthology *Seeds of Fire* was released under the same title.[5] My translations of Bei Dao's grim story "Thirteen Happiness Street" and the poems "The Answer," "All," and "The Old Temple," plus a synopsis of *The Yellow Earth*, became part of both editions.

***

Old Snow was published by New Directions in New York in 1991 and by Anvil Press Poetry in London in 1992. One welcome innovation shared by these twin publications was bilingual texts on facing pages, in response to new exiles like Bei Dao as well as overseas Chinese readers around the world. Different but similarly appreciative accounts of the author appear on the back cover along with photos of the author taken by Shao Fei. The Anvil Press edition features brief notes on the author and the co-translators on the final page. I wrote a terse introductory preface for both titles, much shorter than for their predecessor.

As before, the poems themselves are not dated but are arranged in three chronological parts: part 1: Berlin (eight poems), part 2: Oslo (ten), and part 3: Stockholm (twenty). Naming these sections for the cities where Bei Dao lived between 1989 and 1991 is an eloquent comment on his statelessness at this time, living in Europe and unable to return to his family back in China. It's possible that without the pressure exerted on him by his friends and colleagues abroad he might have returned home regardless of the personal danger he'd be risking. The most tender but also the saddest poem in this collection is "A Picture," subtitled "for Tiantian's fifth birthday," a birthday at which he could not be present. This poem was chosen by the editors of the UK's Poetry Society to be featured in Poems on the Underground (a program showcasing poetry in London Tube train carriages) in 1991 and to be included in its 1993 edition of the anthology *Poems on the Underground*. This is just one example of how the poems in *Old Snow* attracted readers far beyond the small circle of teachers and researchers of modern Chinese literature.

The choice of "Old Snow" as the title poem in the new collection was made for several reasons: not only its sonority in English but also for its evocation of life in snowbound Oslo colored by Bei Dao's isolation from his family in Beijing. The "green frogs" and "postmen's strike" in the poems refer to Oslo postmen, who wore green uniforms for their deliveries and observed Norway's Christian heritage by halting work for four or five days over Easter, cutting off any chance of letters from home or even international newspapers. Living in the cramped quarters of a student hostel, Bei Dao felt stranded, left even more isolated as Norway's national borders are obliterated by the snow. Overall, the tone of this collection is bleak. The poems are shorter and fewer than his earlier poetry; words are little compensation for the terrible landscapes that pervaded his memories and haunted his present. In a way that now seems fitting, this is the last collection of poems from China I've translated.

Translating He Qifang's poems in the 1970s, I was aware of sharing a fine sort of melancholy with him only to find his dream becoming a nightmare that was beyond my experience. For him, there was no way to avoid or escape disaster until he learned to follow a different path. Bei Dao, under these terrible circumstances, wrote poetry that was impassioned, wanting the world to be better but not believing it ever would be; as his translator, I inevitably absorbed his choices and responses.

The idea of a Bei Dao archive surfaced several years later, after I'd moved to Hong Kong in 2006 and has now materialized; it is to be joined with a similar Chen Kaige archive; thanks are due to the University Librarian, Louise Jones, whose tactful and expert contribution was essential to both. Meanwhile, my own attention was diverted in another direction: fiction, not poetry, set in the remote and impoverished southwest border and first composed in the mid-1980s; this translation raised a whole set of different questions.

Notes

1. The note on the verso page states that of these poems, forty-one were included in *Notes from the City of Sun*; nine were in *Renditions* in 1983 and reprinted in *Trees on the Mountain*; fourteen appeared in the *Bulletin of Concerned Asian Scholars* in 1984 and in *Contemporary Chinese Literature*, edited by Michael S. Duke in 1985. All are thanked for releasing copyright for this edition.
2. The original story was published in *Jintian* 5 (1979). My translation was first published in *Bulletin of Concerned Asian Scholars* in 1984; an expanded version headed the list of contents in from the *Bulletin* in *Contemporary Chinese Literature*, 9–10.
3. *Renditions* 26 (Autumn 1986), 1987.
4. Wan Zhi [Chen Maiping], "Ju san li he, dou yi cheng liu shui luo hua: zhuiji 'Jintian' haiwai fukan chuqi de jici bian weihui yi" [Gathered, they scattered; the divided now join; all become rivers in stream and blossoms in fall: retrospective notes on the editorial meetings of Today's overseas edition].
5. See chapter 8 for an example of the anthology's reception in China.

Chapter 10

The King of Fiction in Two Places

It was not my idea to translate Ah Cheng's stories. In fact, this undertaking started with hesitation, then met with gratitude, followed by ignominy, and finally competition with another version. Squeezed in between, from my perspective as translator, came the need to justify distinctly different English vocabularies (official jargon and young men's slang), the construction and naming of characters, and the choice of title, the trickiest of all. It's possible for living writers and their translators to enjoy the closest relationships, but they can also be distant; others who intervene in the author's work are sometimes welcomed and sometimes not. Presented in three different forms in three different books, none of the three translations (described later) can be characterized as fully satisfactory. Self-righteous complaints (examples of which are in chapter 8) are rarely worth retelling, but it remains some comfort that this narrative has been an isolated case in my translation history.

***

In late 1984, I was approached by former colleagues at the Foreign Languages Press asking if I would be willing to translate a short story published earlier that year that was causing a sensation in the literary world. The story was "Qi wang" 棋王 (The king of chess) by a hitherto unknown author writing under the pen name Ah Cheng. With some regret, I turned down the offer on the grounds that I knew little, if anything, about any form of chess, European or Chinese.

Two years later, after I'd left the Foreign Languages Press and moved to the nearby College of Foreign Affairs, I received a letter from Ah Cheng's literary agent, Tan Shih-Ying of Transworld Media Associates in Hong Kong, suggesting that I translate the three stories that had by 1985 been published as "The King of Chess," "Shu wang" (The king of trees) and "Haizi wang" (The king of children), which I did for a collection, *Three Kings*. Professionally, the author always appeared under his pen name Ah Cheng; his formal name is Zhong Acheng. His father was well-known in literary and academic circles, and his mother, I'd been told, was "a big shot" at Beijing Film Studio.

My friends in China were pleased that I had been offered this task and spoke warmly about the writer. After some hesitation, I decided to accept. How was I to know that this decision was to lead to the most complicated, difficult, and troublesome translating that I've ever encountered. I soon found that although knowledge of Chinese chess was not essential, the texts were quite difficult, written in a colloquial but carefully controlled style, unlike anything I had previously translated.

Another problem, which for me at least was not a minor one, was the length of what might be called the translation unit: in contrast to poetry and letters, I found it cumbersome in long fiction to make more or less arbitrary distinctions on what constituted a self-contained unit. It was just as well that these three items were only long short stories, but their length remained a problem throughout. The draft-after-draft process that I'd adopted for translating poetry was barely workable, and I never managed to invent a new process.

To cope with these problems, I coaxed Ren Xiaoping, a teacher at the College of Foreign Affairs, to prepare an initial draft of "The King of Children" and Zhuang Nanbing, a graduate student I'd been supervising, to take on "The King of Trees." Zhuang also assisted with "The King of Chess." Before the translations were completed, I'd moved to Oslo, where I also received assistance from Chen Maiping as well as from Halvor Eifring, my colleague at the University of Oslo, and my husband Anders. To my regret, I haven't been able to contact Ren Xiaoping and Zhuang Nanbing since the book was published in London in 1990 or on its republication in New York under a different title twenty years later. Should either of them happen to come across my current address in Sydney, I urge them to get in touch.

What has remained uncertain is how we three translators should be recognized. It's not always easy to determine whether someone should be credited as a co-translator or as someone whose help is acknowledged in a note preceding the main text. Very roughly, if the original-language (in this case, Chinese) speaker drafts a version in which relatively few changes need be contributed by the translation-language (in this case, English) speaker then it should be regarded as a case of co-translation. On the other hand, if the original-language speaker makes a rough draft that requires extensive or even complete rewriting with reference to the original by the translation-language speaker, then the original-language speaker is only owed a place in the acknowledgements. Unfortunately, I've no way of knowing whether Ren Xiaoping and Zhuang Nanbing thought of themselves as co-translators of *Three Kings* or just as being owed a grateful acknowledgement; in any case, it should have been decided while all of three us were still in Beijing and well before publication.

***

Not surprisingly, because Ah Cheng had already achieved fame on the mainland, Hong Kong publishers responded enthusiastically to my inquiries, including *Renditions* in 1987 and The Chinese University Press early in 1988; several publishers in the US and elsewhere were also asking about the possible publication of my translation. As I should have realized earlier, however, my role as translator in this case did not include negotiating publication.

In September 1988, I received a letter from Guido Waldman, writing for Collins Harvill Publishers in London. Tan had let them know that I had in hand an English translation of *Three Kings*, and because Collins Harvill was negotiating the acquisition of the publication rights, they would be very pleased to see my translation as soon as possible. This was, of course, a very attractive opportunity, and I was happy to acquiesce.

In 1979, Harvill's new publisher, Christopher MacLehose,[1] had turned the firm into one of the UK's most respected publishers of translated fiction, and it in turn had recently been acquired by Collins, one of the UK's biggest publishers. My correspondence was directly with the editor, who was also an accomplished translator; he mentioned that he'd been considering an English version after reading the French translation, presumably also via Ah Cheng's agent.

The offer to me from Collins Harvill was generous, including both a flat fee and royalties. The contract was signed in February 1989, passing all copyright to Collins. An apparently regular paragraph in the contract noted that the publishers would ensure "that the name of the translator shall appear with appropriate prominence on the title page of every copy of the said translation." On publication I was pleased to find my name as translator and author of an introduction on the inside back jacket as well.

Waldman turned out to be a discreet and thoughtful editor. In April 1989, he wrote to warn me that "living outside England for so long, your ear may not be any more wholly attuned to current speech rhythms

The King of Fiction in Two Places 145

here, and we do want to avoid a version that reads too much like an American one." He was dead right, and I took no offense. I already knew that Australian English was more like US English than London English. I also hadn't lived in an English-speaking country since 1980; I'd spent four years in Cambridge, Massachusetts, and only a year in London back in 1975. He also suggested "a somewhat toned-down version" of my introduction and enclosed a page of tactfully worded comments. I set about adopting his suggestions.

One of his proposals was for the nickname "Kneeballs" for a character in "The King of Chess" to be changed to "Longstaff," a word which to me sounded almost archaic; after some experimentation, we compromised on "Tall Balls," a phrase I still enjoy reading. I also recall a longish correspondence about the most appropriate term for the long knife that plays a prominent role in "The King of Trees." Despite some misgivings, I adopted Waldman's suggestion of "machete." It wasn't until the end of May 1989 that I returned the amended translation and supporting materials; he responded with his usual courtesy. I owe much to his editing and remain deeply grateful for it. There was some discussion of prospective US publishers, "many of whom [had] already expressed interest," but nothing came of this over the next decade.

The translation was released in early 1990 under the title *Three Kings: Three Stories from Today's China*. The timing, not long after the June Fourth massacres of 1989, was inevitably poor.[2] It was particularly unfortunate, in my eyes, that the book's cover illustration was a detail from an idyllic landscape painting in the style of Zhao Mengfu (a Yuan-dynasty scholar painter) by Wang Cheming in 1670. Compounding this was the front cover flap's introduction, which began with "these three enchanting novellas..." and concluded with the description "a masterpiece of wry compassion." This is not how I would characterize the individual stories or the book as a whole. I also began to wonder if my tactic in featuring initial capital letters and an extended glossary was too fussy or interfering for the kind of reader I'd envisaged as appreciating Ah Cheng's subtle meanings.

***

Since 1980, I'd grown accustomed to translating poetry and fiction by people I already knew, often close friends. My acknowledgments for *Three Kings* thanked Ah Cheng, Chen Maiping, and Anders "for their continued support and help throughout this project"; it would have been more accurate to indicate I had little direct contact with Ah Cheng. Our first encounter was in Beijing in August 1987, but I don't have a record of our conversation except that it was brief. By 1988, he'd moved to the US, and Gladys Yang passed on the news that he was living very frugally in a trailer, doing odd jobs and reveling in his freedom. When I'd finished the first draft, I mailed him a copy. In his reply, he explained a few items, such as the saying "If you've rice in the bin for the following day, To be king of children is not worth the pay" (meaning that only the poor become teachers), and his use of the term "white sunshine" in contrast to "red sunshine."[3] Many years later, in November 2007, at a symposium organized by the Macau Ricci Institute that was attended by a large number of contemporary Chinese writers, I was brought over to meet Ah Cheng in person for the first time since our encounter in 1987. We briefly greeted each other. I've never seen him again or had any other contact. My admiration for his writing remains high.

Whether it was the timing or for some other reason, the book's reception was deeply disappointing. The royalty statements from Collins Harvill tell a sad tale: sales figures showed that the enchanting descriptions were hardly noticed by a readership outside China. In 1995, MacLehose returned Harvill to its earlier independence; by that time, sales of *Three Kings* had shrunk to fewer than a handful, and my generous advance remained unearned. Harvill Press was acquired by Random House in 2002, and in 2008, I received my last statement from them, showing no

The King of Fiction in Two Places

copies sold. The book was now out of print, there were no plans for reissue, and the translation rights reverted to me.

There was some good news. Apart from Bei Dao's poetry and fiction, and like most other new Chinese books in English around that time, few reviews were featured by the English-language press, but those passed over to me were generally favorable. I was especially pleased to find a review in the *Far Eastern Economic Review*,[4] then the most comprehensive and well-reported weekly newspaper on East Asia. The reviewer Don Cohn claimed that "The Chess Master" was a better title, ignoring the awkward fact that "master" was not applicable to the other two stories. (I've also seen the title given as "The Chess Champion.") The real problem, however, was the title that I'd chosen myself: *Three Kings*. Thanks to my militantly atheist upbringing, I was completely unaware that the term "Three Kings" referred to one of Christianity's most sacred events. It came as a shock to find the existence of a huge number of publications using "three kings" as or in a title, and I've occasionally wondered whether any readers have been shocked by what they found in this book.

The honorific term "king" is common enough in Chinese to suggest outstanding competence as in, for example, the phrase "king of dumplings." However, it's not a common usage in English, and a browsing reader in an English-language bookshop most likely would never take it to mean a story (or stories) about China. The title "The Chess Master" is more idiomatic but fails to make a link with the other two stories with matching titles: "The Tree Master" and "The Children's Master" are both too awkward to complete the trio. In short, I still don't know what the title should be.

***

The texts on which the translation of the three stories were eventually based are those in the book *Qi wang*[5] and differ slightly from the original versions published in Beijing-based literary journals. The stories are set in a remote, mountainous area in southwest China, and the main characters are educated (or semi-educated) young men and women who have been displaced from their homes in north China; it's not spelled out exactly where their family lived, but it can be understood that they are from Beijing (as were Ah Cheng and Chen Kaige). As discussed in chapter 8 in relation to Chen Kaige's film *The King of Children* (my translation of the film title), they were officially designated as *zhishi qingnian*, an expression usually abbreviated as *zhiqing*, and the standard translation "educated youth" and abbreviation "EYs" are adopted in the *Three Kings* translation and explained in the glossary.

Before tackling the main text, I faced questions on how to translate the author's name, the title, and the names of the characters in the first story. At the time there was never any likelihood of using the author's formal name, Zhong Acheng 鍾阿城, a matter I now regret. I was presented first with the correct FLP version of the author's pen name: A Cheng. The vowels *a*, *i*, and *o* are in principle free-standing romanizations, but adding an *h* after *a* and *o* lessens the ambiguity to English-language readers; in this case, it also gives a closer approximation of the actual pronunciation. So, the author became Ah Cheng. There was still the problem that readers may think either "Ah" or "Cheng" was his surname, making it crucial that the front cover, the title page, and every mention in the introduction all contained the full two syllables.[6]

The Chinese title for the book edition, *Qi wang*, would have appealed to Chinese readers, but I wasn't at all sure that *The King of Chess* would have the same association for English-language readers, so at an early stage in correspondence with Tan Shih-Ying, *Three Kings* was adopted for the title. In hindsight, I've wondered about the use of the word "king" in English and Chinese. The word *wang* is close in meaning to English "king": both refer to the ruler of a country but also are also used colloquially for a person who excels in a particular activity. There's an old English proverb, dating back to the sixteenth century or earlier, "in the country of the blind, the one-eyed man is king." The meaning can be interpreted in a number of different ways, but one interpretation is that kingship designates a person possessing superior knowledge or ability and therefore not in the same category as his subjects. The word *wang* has a similar connotation when it occurs in colloquial discourse, as in "dumpling king" or "king of dumpling" as seen in restaurant names. When I see such phrases, I mentally change the name into "the king of dumplings," on the grounds that such kings are not dumplings themselves. Ah Cheng's story titles use *wang* in much the same colloquial way.

I've always held that the English version of the three titles should share the same structure in translation: that is, starting with a definite article for the first noun and ending with the final noun in the plural (except in the case of the chess king). Thus: "The King of Chess," "The King of Trees," and "The King of Children." Four English versions of the last story title are theoretically possible: King of Children; King of the Children; The King of Children; and The King of the Children. Only the third variant specifically implies that the kings themselves are not in the same category as their subjects, whereas the second implies that the king is one of the children. Nevertheless, three of these versions have been used in published translations of "Haizi wang." In other words, the translators (or their editors) may have chosen what seems to them to be best for sales rather than an echo or promise of the story's meaning.

A. S. Byatt touches on a similar dilemma in her introduction to a new edition of her novel *The Shadow of The Sun*. It was first published under the title *Shadow of a Sun*, suggested by poet Cecil Day-Lewis because, according to Byatt, "[this] title would sound better."[7] Gladys Yang's translation of Ah Cheng's "Shu wang" for the FLP appeared as "King of Trees" (presumably on the grounds that shorter is better; also, it may not have been her own choice).[8] I would argue that a person nicknamed "the king of children" is an adult who presides over the children in his care, whereas one might expect a "king of the children" to be one of the children (i.e., unlike "king of dumplings").

***

There are several well-known strategies in literary translation for the names of characters, the currently most obnoxious one being only to translate the personal names of the female characters. My preferred choice is to translate characters' informal personal names or nicknames, if a reasonable translation can be found, but not to translate formal personal names or surnames. In "The King of Children," for instance, the nickname "Lao Gan" for the main character appears in the story only once, when he's addressed by Laidi, the only female character who plays an active role in the story.

Because Lao Gan is both the chief character and the first-person narrator, it seemed worthwhile to translate his nickname, although it took me some time to settle on Beanpole. Strictly speaking, the term "the king of children" only applies to Beanpole by the end of the story. He'd already been at the labor camp for seven years and had also finished three years at secondary school, giving him an advantage over the other boys in the labor camp who'd only managed to finish primary school. Nevertheless, it was only when he became a true teacher that he achieved this more respectful and affectionate title.

In the same story, one EY is named Lao Hei; others likely have nicknames as well, but he is the only one whose nickname is mentioned. Because the word "hei" can mean both brown or black, and because "Blackie" is blatantly racist, I adopted "Brownie," despite it sharing a name with the chocolate treats. The only other named character among the young men and women in the camp is the cook, Laidi 来弟. Her name means roughly "let a little brother come" and is given to girls in a family lacking male descendants. This seemed too complicated to explain in a single word, so I left it untranslated. It's a pity, though: the name partly explains her aggressive attitude toward the young men in the camp. The author (perhaps remembering the woman Laidi was based on) at least portrayed her as clever in two ways: one, she could compose music, which none of the boys could do; two, she's sexually more active than the boys.

The most lavish praise for "Qi wang" has been for the extraordinarily detached stance of the characters, especially the narrators, toward the terrible political, economic, and social upheavals of the Cultural Revolution; they treat these as a part of life that's unpleasant but may be endured at minimal cost. One manifestation of this style is its apparent simplicity because, as mentioned before, the author doesn't intervene in the story with elaborate explanations or colorful stylistic devices. The narrative consists of descriptions of action and dialogue: no emotions are described, and there are no direct attacks on corruption and hardship: the discourse is flat, so that portrayals of suffering and tragedy are more effective. The narrative veers between traditional literary word patterns and contemporary colloquial speech, although even the more contemporary-sounding colloquial effects tend to be reminiscent of traditional storyteller fiction; as one critic noticed, there are no signs of polishing, but much is conveyed through the choice of words.[9] This quality was especially evident in "The King of Chess," and given this clear guidance I attempted to reproduce the same effect. Whether or not I achieved it, it may still be the case that most English-language readers would not see, or fail to understand, why these two different voices were present. It wasn't easy to find the appropriate language and illustrations to effect these indirect messages. Ah Cheng himself has claimed that he learned how to tell stories in order to earn a meal. There is, however, no particular reason why his readers should accept this claim at face value.

A telling example comes from an anecdote Ah Cheng related about his life in Xishuangbanna. Although his father was a distinguished writer and critic, the family had become desperately poor since their fall from grace, and so sending money or goods to support Ah Cheng's semi-exile was out of the question. Instead, he and his companions would descend on the local village for a meal to supplement their meagre rations (such excursions are mentioned in "The King of Chess"). In order to pay for his meals, Ah Cheng became a storyteller, sometimes adapting European novels from his father's bookshelves for a Chinese audience. One of these novels was *Anna Karenina*, whose story, which I was told became sinified for this purpose, took several months to complete. In 1984, on a visit back to the village after he'd become famous, the villagers confronted him with some hostility, having by then seen on local television the British adaptation of the original novel. The implied message in this anecdote is that an author's role lies not only in revealing human resilience in the face of bitter fate but also in meeting readers' expectations. It also signals to the translator that their narrative language had to cope with both strict simplicity and fundamental truths of existence. Although to some extent this demand was also present in Bei Dao's poetry and Chen Maiping's fiction, I found it a uniquely difficult balance in Ah Cheng's work.

***

Another flawed strategy, it turned out, was providing before the main text an academically oriented eighteen-page introduction to the translation, analyzing at length the background of the stories, the complex reception it provoked, and its literary innovations. Another device that may have discouraged readers was spelling with an initial capital in the translation itself the large number of political terms and other set phrases current during the Cultural Revolution and often meaning the opposite of what would normally be understood, and then finally providing a seven-page glossary at the back of the book explaining their meaning. (Perry Link had a similar glossary in his 1983 *Stubborn Weeds*.)

In hope that these stories might attract a readership outside Chinese studies, I also included brief notes on traditional Chinese concepts and literary works in the glossary. This specialist vocabulary, for which I adopted (as described in the introduction of the book) a "slightly unnatural English," also appeared in the main text with initial capital letters, prompting the reader to look for the meaning of the term in the glossary, and obviating the need for explanations or glosses in the text or for recourse to footnotes.

Providing some sort of readers' guide had been my consistent policy in translation since the 1970s, its main purpose being to avoid footnotes in the translated text. As far as I am aware, however, my strategy of capitalizing jargon and providing a glossary for Ah Cheng's stories either passed unnoticed or was regarded with distaste, with one notable exception. British academic, poet, novelist, and critic D. J. Enright, one of my literary heroes, praised this choice in a review of the book: "The translator has done well to convey their stiffness by capitalizing jargon and slogans…This device gives edge to the narrator's deadpan mention that his parents had fallen foul of the authorities."

It was not only general readers who found the book marginal, to put it politely. Subsequent academic research in English on Ah Cheng's fiction also ignored both the translation and the introduction. My habit of writing lengthy introductions to translations remained in place, however, for at least two more decades.

***

The FLP was not too dismayed that I didn't accept its offer to translate Ah Cheng's stories in 1984. A bilingual edition under the bilingual titles *A Cheng xiaoshuo xuan* and *Selected Stories by A Cheng* appeared in August 1999, containing "The Chess Master," translated by W. J. F. Jenner and "King of Trees," translated by Gladys Yang, plus three other stories. Still, my translation had been vindicated in one way: after an exhaustive comparison of the two versions of "The King of Chess," Li Yi, now a lecturer at Beijing International Studies University, concluded that I had employed a broader vocabulary resulting in a more accurate translation.[10]

Although I admired Ah Cheng's achievements, I was glad I'd finished the stories and declared in a letter to Gladys Yang that I was absolutely not ever going to translate any more of his work. It wasn't that I disliked what he wrote, but I wasn't wholly impressed by his underlying messages;

in any case, I was still not happy about translating fiction. I confessed to Gladys that I stole several phrases from her own translation of "King of Trees" and was tempted to steal others as well but restrained myself. Even with my theft, however, I did produce a more literal version of the work, and I reasoned that if it was tough on the readers, it was just too bad. I didn't see the book being a bestseller anyway.

My gloom was justified. *Three Kings* at least managed to attract the attention of the Department of Language Engineering at the Centre for Translation Studies at the University of Manchester Institute of Science and Technology in July 1999, which seemed to be very keen to include it in their Translational English Corpus. I was very willing to cooperate, of course, and filled in their questionnaire as requested, but I've heard nothing further from them. Another quite different opportunity to engage with Ah Cheng's fiction came when Chen Kaige decided to film "The King of Children." Its mixed reception is discussed in chapter 8.

***

A new offer for the stories' publication came from New Directions early in the new century. By this time, New Directions had a growing Chinese literature list and was the main international publisher of Bei Dao's poetry, so I was optimistic about the outcome. First, a different book title was chosen: *The King of Trees*. This was partly for the sake of differentiating between the two different publications, but it also underlined the collection's environmental message.

More problematic was the editor's intervention in the translation itself. A characteristic of Ah Cheng's writing that was particularly celebrated by its Chinese readers is the adoption of a standard technique from traditional Chinese fiction: indicating thoughts and emotions not through the author's direct access to the character's mind but their small, often inadvertent gestures, such as stroking, patting, scratching, or smoothing the hair on their head. To work out which Chinese words meant which kind of action and in turn which kind of thought or emotion was thereby

The King of Fiction in Two Places

conveyed wasn't always evident to me, and I was obliged to find a Chinese friend (usually Chen Maiping) who would tell me what they meant.

To the New Directions editor, however, these depictions were simply meaningless to US readers, and accordingly substantial cuts were made of such passages. I was in some cases allowed to maintain the original text or modify it only slightly, but for the most part I accepted that the editor enjoyed an expert understanding of his readers and I didn't. My elaborate device of using initial capital letters for set words and phrases was also discarded, and my introduction was abbreviated and relegated to the back of the book. At least the definite article heading the title was retained: it became *The King of Trees*.

***

Despite its rewriting, this version of Ah Cheng's three stories was still not welcome to readers. Again, the cover depiction of graceful blossoms on branches as in traditional Chinese painting was (in my opinion, which was not sought) irrelevant, if not actually misleading, to the understanding of the issues raised in Ah Cheng's fiction. But the book did reach an audience in the two years after its publication. My royalty statements show a respectable number of sold copies, nearly three hundred in 2013, rising to nearly ten thousand in 2014, half of which were exported. I don't have figures for 2015, but only 236 copies were sold in 2016 and about the same for 2017. By way of contrast, nine copies of Bei Dao's *Old Snow* were sold in 2013, eighteen copies in 2014, zero for 2016, and eighteen again in 2017. I'd guess that these sales went to the UK more than to the US because there were more students taking modern Chinese literature courses there. It comes as no surprise that fiction outsold poetry.

***

I have mentioned previously Ah Cheng's apparent disinclination to entertain the idea that he, as the writer, and I, as his translator, might meet in person or in correspondence. You, my dear reader, might also judge that in the absence of close contact, only my pride was injured, and you may be right. It also may well be the case that my translation strategies or level of competence in English, Chinese, or both were at fault. If so, it would then be not only Ah Cheng who had reason to distrust me; his potential readers would also have had grounds to feel aggrieved. On the other hand, it could be that Ah Cheng's style erects an invisible but impenetrable barrier to his English-language readers. On reflection, it would probably have been better for me if I had honored my reluctance to accept the initial offer from the Foreign Languages Press.

None of this reflects on Ah Cheng's work, of course. What remains, from first to last, is the repeated assurance by my friends and colleagues that Ah Cheng's three "king" stories are among the best, if not the best, fiction produced in China in the 1980s. To the present day, Ah Cheng continues to write and to be regarded with the greatest respect. It would not be the first time that readers' expectations differed across national language boundaries or that poor translation disguised a remarkable achievement.

This whole experience, too, serves to underline the importance of personal contact, or even just being on the ground, when it comes to securing material that any translator would covet. It is also manifestly the case that personal contact can be disrupted by all sorts of unexpected developments. It's also worth letting other people know that motives may be mixed; intentions differ and clash, and the whole picture is rarely clear.

In a generous gesture shortly after publication of *The King of Trees*, the publisher of New Directions recommended me to the Santa Maddalena Foundation near Florence for a six-week residential fellowship in June–July 2011.[11] It was there that I wrote an introduction to Dung Kai-cheung's *Atlas*, published in 2012 (and the subject of chapter 14). During my residence, I took the opportunity to suggest to the director of the foundation, Beatrice Monti della Corte, inviting one of three writers, Bei Dao (then resident in Hong Kong), Dung Kai-cheung, or Leung Ping-kwan to take up a fellowship. Although at that point rather few contemporary

The King of Fiction in Two Places 157

PRC authors would have been able to meet the foundation's emphasis on social interaction, these three writers from Hong Kong would have fully qualified. As far as I know, nothing happened. Leung Ping-kwan, perhaps the best choice, sadly died two years later.

***

Thinking back on these years, I've often wondered why both versions of Ah Cheng's fiction were unsuccessful in becoming profitable. I am tempted to claim that the publishers' heavy editorial revisions in both cases may have inhibited an appreciation of the translatee's distinctive style. It is also possible that poetry was more suited to my writing style than fiction. I'd by then lost my native dialect (Australian English) from moving from country to country, being mostly enmeshed in academic work and the company of academics from many different places; now, I accepted the necessity throughout most of my adult life to be polylingual.

In consequence, I'd developed a formal style that suited well enough the comparatively formal tone characteristic of Chinese poetry up until the end of the twentieth century. Dialogue, in contrast, especially colloquial and vernacular discourse, was not among my strengths. To correct this, I became even more obsessive about reading fiction written in English by native speakers for at least a couple of hours every day. It sometimes happened that the puzzles I encountered in teaching or translating during the day would be solved in the book I read later that same day. I prudently extended my reading, where possible, to morning and late-night hours as well. Still, even after we moved to Scotland in 1990, it didn't occur to me that English in any part of Britain was not my native dialect.

***

Four years teaching at the University of Oslo while translating *Three Kings* wasn't a happy experience for me, and I spent much of my time visiting China and exchanging letters (which I can only describe as homesick) with Gladys Yang, my most affectionate and dedicated respondent in the years 1986 to 1990. Up to 1989, Gladys and Xianyi enjoyed a never-ending sequence of visits from Chinese writers, Western sinologists, and publishers from around the world. Although we could all see the signs, most of us (Bei Dao being an exception) expected that the growing unease in national politics would be resolved as it had in the case of the "spiritual pollution" movement in 1983. We were wrong.

Notes

1. I met MacLehose in person at a UNESCO-based conference in Beijing in 2009, where his wife was giving a paper. It was a good opportunity to pass on my gratitude for dealings with Harvill.
2. The term "Tiananmen event/massacre," commonly used in the English-language press, is misleading because Tiananmen Square was not the only place where large demonstrations were brutally suppressed; the term used in Chinese refers to the date in 1989 when the movement had reached its peak and was then destroyed in cities throughout China.
3. Letter dated April 8, 1988.
4. Don Cohn, "We Three Kings from Orient Are," *Far Eastern Economic Review*, November 8, 1990, p. 40.
5. Ah Cheng, *Qi wang* (Beijing: Zuojia chubanshe, 1985).
6. It's not uncommon, still, to find "Zedong" given as Mao Zedong's surname in the daily press. Some habits are hard to break. Still, I've never seen a Mr. Ah or a Mr. Cheng for Ah Cheng.
7. Byatt, xiii. The original publication was by Chatto & Windus in 1964.
8. Pallavi Singhal, "How to win the Miles Franklin Award," 2–3.
9. Li Ziyun, "Huashuo Ah Cheng."
10. I'd been invited to visit Shanghai Jiaotong University in 2016 on the initiative of Li Yi, then a graduate student. See also her article 'Jiyu yuliaoku de 'Qi wang' yingyi benfan yifenge bijiao yanjiu; A Corpus-based Comparative Study on the Translation Style of Two English Versions of Qi Wang" *Shandong Foreign Language Teaching* 41 no. 1 (2020).
11. The full name of the foundation is The Gregor von Rezzori and Beatrice Monti della Corte Retreat for Writers.

CHAPTER 11

TRANSLATION DISTRACTIONS

Since my earlier visit, I thought of the University of Edinburgh as a conservative institution famous for medicine, religion, and law. I was soon to discover that a group of skilled arts faculty was forming an unexpected hub for translation studies. A colleague in an adjacent department, Şebnem Susam-Saraeva, was appointed solely on her research and teaching in translation studies, and an unexpected influx of students from China, Taiwan, and other parts of Asia were presenting their research subjects on various aspects of translation. We in Chinese studies were especially affected, and we began teaching translation to undergraduates and supervising postgraduates in translation research. While I was still living in Oslo, I had written a long article on some aspects of translation that I'd encountered in China,[1] and a few years later I wrote a more bad-tempered article in a linguistically oriented journal that promptly folded.[2] I was finding the new translation theories to be an opening to new and demanding ways of looking not just at translation but also at cross-cultural studies more generally. However, my education took hold slowly.

It was also in Edinburgh that I found new texts to translate: fiction written by Chinese women. I'd translated some poems by women for the FLP's magazine *Chinese Literature*, and I knew several of the writers, but

I can't think of any particular reason why my translation choices mostly hadn't included writing by women. In November 1986 I'd received a letter from a former colleague in the FLP's English Books section who was now transferred to the Chinese Literature section, asking me to contribute translations of new women poets as a Panda Book. I had previously been asked to translate some of Shu Ting's poems but hadn't been keen, and I also turned down FLP's invitation.

Don Cohn wrote to me in early 1987 about a new issue of *Renditions* on Chinese women writers, suggesting a dozen women writers among whom I could choose, but although I knew their work, I was not particularly impressed. In addition, I was already overcommitted to other writers. However, I'd become uneasy about not having translated more women writers earlier and with more conviction. The breakthrough came with an invitation to translate recent fiction by Wang Anyi.

***

At the beginning of the 1980s, Wang Anyi had emerged as a promising young writer with an impeccable background (her mother was a well-known left-wing writer from the 1950s and 1960s) and a special interest in women's experiences in the newly relaxed atmosphere following the end of the Cultural Revolution. Her trilogy dating 1986–1987, however, opened up new territory: at a time when exploring sexual relationships between young men and women in fiction was still taboo, Wang Anyi depicted extramarital affairs in three novellas: *Romance on a Barren Mountain* (*Huangshan zhi lian* 荒山之恋), *Romance in a Small Town* (*Xiao cheng zhi lian* 小城之恋), and *Romance in Brocade Valley* (*Jinxiugu zhi lian* 锦绣谷之恋). In all three, the heroine is the dominant partner in the relationship; in *Romance in Brocade Valley*, the last and most controversial, a young married woman establishes her own identity through a brief (and apparently imaginary) affair.

New Directions had approached me in the late 1980s to translate *Romance in Brocade Valley*. I was living in Norway and collaborating with

Chen Maiping as a co-translator, and with his agreement to continue our partnership, I accepted the invitation and read the Chinese text with some trepidation. I still wasn't very sure of how I would manage fiction, which remained something of an experiment for me. But in those days, I found it difficult to turn down an offer from a prominent New York publisher. I was also aware, before I finally agreed to accept this task, that English translations of the two earlier novellas had already been published in *Renditions*, although I was unable able to find out why this third novella was still untranslated. Another source of unease was that New Directions decreed a simplified title, *Brocade Valley*. I'd had some reluctance about this because the amended title cut this third and closing volume from the sequence. However, I signed the contract in 1990, and the translation was published in 1992.

As I began the preliminary drafts, it soon became evident that fiction translation was in some ways (and contrary to public wisdom) more difficult than poetry translation. To start, there were several voices that needed to be re-created: male and female, young and old, famous and ordinary. Another issue was the translation of people's names, jobs, and location, as well as formal and informal terms of address. These matters had not been a problem with Bei Dao's six stories and even less with Ah Cheng's three, in which formal personal names were usually replaced by nicknames and office jobs were not part of the narrative.

The heroine of *Brocade Valley* works as a manuscript editor of a leading publisher in Shanghai and manages to secure an invitation to a writers' conference about to take place at a famous beauty spot and tourist attraction, Brocade Valley. Among other benefits, going to this conference would mean some welcome space from her husband, with whom she shares a one-room apartment with a kitchen alcove consisting of a two-burner gas stove and cold running water; shared toilets and lavatories are located down the corridor outside for communal use. Her office is similarly dingy: every morning the editors are obliged to dust their own desks and fetch their thermos of hot water from boilers in the basement. (These details were familiar to me from my spell at the FLP.)

For this story, Wang Anyi was ready to experiment with different styles and voices. Her heroine occupies a triple persona: she is narrator, protagonist, and inhabitant of a future world, so dominant that the secondary characters (both male: her boring husband and the glamorous writer) are reduced to reflections of her thoughts and emotions. Her romance is playfully uncertain: wisps of his cigarette smoke hold deep, ambiguous meanings, and her return to everyday domesticity is like waking from a dream.

As mentioned earlier, it's my practice to avoid footnotes in literary texts, providing instead explanations in a preface or glossary, or by manipulating the main text (such as when I capitalized jargon in *Three Kings*). In this case, I wrote an introduction with some general explanations on the setting for readers not familiar with Chinese society at the time set out in the narrative. Much of the informal language common in China in the 1970s and 1980s had been replaced at the end of the 1980s, and creating equivalents that both reflected the period and were clear to present-day Anglophone readers proved more complicated than I'd thought.

One of the trickiest examples of changes in conversational Chinese speech was the conventional terminology used at the time for addressing one's colleagues. Two key terms were *lao* 老 (literally meaning "old" but used roughly as a prefix for colleagues who were male, older, senior, or physically larger, translated as "Mr.") and *xiao* 小 (meaning both "young" and "small," used for colleagues who were female, younger, junior, or physically smaller, translated as Miss). At the time of writing, these terms suggested the formality and tensions in offices where colleagues had often been obliged to inform on each other and rarely formed close personal friendships. The Chinese readers of that time (or even later) needed no explanation, but my task was to explain their secondary meanings to a readership that had scarcely existed a decade earlier.

Several well established devices were helpful. For example, when the heroine is offered a chance to report on the writers' conference, the location is given as Lushan, a place for which to Chinese readers needed no explanation. Most non-Chinese readers, however, would not know it was a renowned scenic spot in a mountain range in central southern China, especially celebrated as the place where Mao Zedong wrote a famous poem dedicated to his wife Jiang Qing. Instead of explaining this in a footnote, I used a trick common in conventional English fiction: the place name (Brocade Valley) is not immediately explained at first mention but rather shortly afterward, while the main character is musing over her good luck in being able to go there.

Another matter seemed to me too delicate to explain in the introduction; I now wish I had. It was common gossip in Chinese literary circles at the time that the famous writer that the heroine encounters at the conference is actually a thinly veiled portrait of a famous novelist known for his obsessive sexual interest in attractive young women. At the time, it seemed preferable to allow the reader to construct an opinion of this character based solely on the text itself.

Finally, a trap more treacherous than any of the previous ones is that fiction translation tends to descend all too easily into clichés and monotonous prose. I found myself falling into barely hidden traps. Because of this, it became even more important to let the early drafts rest for weeks before achieving the distance needed for rewriting.

***

In what would have been their standard procedure, the New Directions editorial staff was inclined to adapt fiction translation to local audiences according to their expert knowledge of their readership. The publisher's editorial staff was thanked, of course, in my introduction, but the editorial process brought about changes that caused me some concern. First, the title was reduced from four words to two: the justification for this was obvious, the publishers being responsible only for a single volume in the trilogy. For academic reasons, nevertheless, I would have preferred to keep the link intact.

Another problem was the excision of much of the excessively wordy prose. Again, the editors had a good case to make. Wang Anyi had developed a very fluid style: paragraphs occupy whole pages, and repetition is frequent. One explanation for this fairly common practice may have been the standard financial arrangement between Chinese writers and their publishers at that time, which was based on the number of characters in the manuscript. Other things being equal (e.g., the writer's fame also being counted as a factor), the longer her manuscript, the more payment the writer could expect. Under those circumstances, who could blame writers for passages such as "She went to the window, walking slowly as she passed the desks of her colleagues, occasionally stopping to ask a question or pass a friendly remark, and reached the window that she opened with both hands, allowing her to glance out at the street below, now being the time of people's daily routines as they milled around, scanning the local food stalls for something special for lunch" (a slightly exaggerated version of Wang Anyi's original) instead of "She crossed over to the window and looked out."

Despite this editing, the translation failed to make an impact on US readers. When a similar fate at the hands of the same publisher met Ah Cheng's fiction, it seemed to me that either I should stop translating fiction or stop trying to have it published in the US. A year later, while I was the acting director of CUHK's Research Centre for Translation (RCT), I attempted to arrange for all three of these novellas to be republished in one volume (or as a set of three) and gained permission to do so from both Wang Anyi and from New Directions. However, in the end, republication never took place.

***

In the meantime, my main translation task was a return to *Letters between Two*, finally to be published in 2000. Then in 2005, as I was nearing compulsory retirement, I was invited to spend a term at the RCT. This led to me quitting my position at the University of Edinburgh and moving to Hong Kong in 2006, yet another step that provided a turning point in my thinking, my practice, and (not to sound more grandiose) my life.

Notes

1. McDougall, "Problems and Possibilities in Translating Contemporary Chinese Literature."
2. McDougall, "Chinese Errors and English Infelicities."

Part V

Hong Kong, Ventlinge, and Sydney

CHAPTER 12

HONG KONG DAZE

Since 2006, I've been concentrating on translating Hong Kong poetry and fiction. It's certainly possible that many of these works were subjected to some kind of self-censorship, although with results more similar to 1940s Shanghai plays than to contemporary mainland literature. At the time, I was only dimly aware of the pressures that bubbled below the surface, beguiled as I was by the professional skills of Hong Kong writers.

My four years living and working in Hong Kong also brought together the practice and research aspects of translation. I'd spent two months in 2005 as a visiting professor at the RCT, the home of *Renditions*.[1] I didn't do much translation there, but a return to a Chinese-speaking environment, even though my Cantonese was nonexistent, was a huge boost: I'd landed in an outrageously fertile cultural environment. The urge to understand translating—what it was, what it could be, and what it should be—resurfaced. The whole atmosphere was energizing.

During those two months, I'd been invited to give talks at CUHK, the Hong Kong Translation Society, the University of Macao, and the Macao Polytechnic Institute: two of these were talks on Chinese concepts of privacy, my most recent research topic; the remaining six were all on different aspects of translation. I remember most clearly the talk I gave to the Hong Kong Translation Society on the realities of translating in mainland China and the pains and gains of poetry translation: I'd thought a lot about both topics before coming to Hong Kong, but the immersion that came with this visit was the first step toward a book that would appear seven years later.

***

At the beginning of 2006 I returned to Hong Kong on a two-year contract as a research professor in the Department of Translation at Chinese University. Translating, conducting research, and teaching became my main activities, thanks to the head of the translation department, Gilbert Fong Chee Fun, a genial colleague who specialized in modern drama translation. The department had an enviable reputation: other staff included Chan Sin-wai, a world leader on computer-aided translation; Li Defeng, a researcher in the new field of cognition in translation practice; and Laurence Wong Kwok-pun (Huang Guobin), a respected poet as well as a skilled translator from French and English into Chinese. They were backed by a magnificently competent administrative team that included Rosalind Chan and Andy Lau. I could not have imagined a more productive body of colleagues and interests.

As if this weren't enough, I was shortly afterward offered the position of acting director of the RCT for three years by the then director, Lawrence W. C. Wong, who was going on long-term leave. I was happy to do this, especially when Anders agreed to take on the post of *Renditions* editor. One of our first tasks was to draw up a comprehensive style guide for contributors and editorial staff; we also commissioned guest editors for the next four issues of *Renditions*. Then and now, we've both been grateful to the RCT permanent staff, Alena Chow, Audrey Heijns, and Cecilia Ip, for their competence, loyalty, and tact.

I'd had the good fortune in 2005 to get to know Professor Wong Nim Yan, one of the outstanding talents in CUHK's Chinese department. The following year, as I was looking for local writing to feature in my new teaching duties, she introduced me to her husband Dung Kai-cheung, as well as several other well-known writers. As I soon discovered, DKC (as we subsequently referred to him) happened to be one of Hong Kong's most gifted writers. My students, both local and mainland, responded enthusiastically to his "Spring Garden Lane" ("Chunyuanjie" 春園街) one of his best-known "essays" (as I then thought them to be) on local history; Nim Yan later became my co-translator for its publication in *Renditions*.[2]

***

Over the next few years, my contributions to *Renditions* included Ding Xilin's *Dear Husband* (co-translated with Flora Lam), a short but brilliantly funny play by one of my favorite May Fourth writers, and *Beijing Sketches* (*Beijing xi mo* 北京戲墨) by Leung Ping-kwan.[3] Next, *The Cold and the Dark* [*Han sen qu* 寒森曲]: extracts" by Pu Songling, which I co-translated with C. D. Alison Bailey, sparked another informal correspondence with Alison, a dear friend since my FLP days, who now taught classical and modern Chinese and researched the presence of severed heads in traditional fiction at the University of British Columbia. Anders and I, along with our colleague Ann Huss, also enjoyed the privilege of attending private coaching in Cantonese conducted with immeasurable aplomb by Hugh Baker; sadly, I never became proficient.

***

In 2009, in another stroke of good luck, I was appointed to the Chinese Literature and Language Department at the City University of Hong Kong in 2009, under the direction of Professor Zhang Longxi, whom I first met in 1981 as Zhu Guangqian's last and most brilliant graduate student. It was here, when Zhang Longxi took sabbatical leave, that I finally became relentlessly exposed to the concept of cross-cultural studies, the subject of a large, lively, and insistent evening class. I also taught more familiar undergraduate classes in translating English to Chinese and Chinese to

English, relying in both cases on materials I'd translated, or otherwise knew well. As had been the case at CUHK, the challenge of a mixed class of Cantonese speakers from Hong Kong and Mandarin speakers from mainland China provided an ideal opportunity to introduce local Hong Kong literature to both groups of students.

Then there was a whole new pleasure in becoming involved with Hong Kong writers. As well as Dung Kai-cheung, other local writers whose work appeared in the translation classes (some of whom afterward also appeared in *Renditions*) included Xi Xi, Leung Ping-kwan, and Xu Xi. Leung Ping-kwan's poems were particularly well received by both mainland and local students. Around this time, at the invitation of my old colleagues at the Foreign Languages Press, I wrote a short, slightly facetious paper on a "pleasure principle" in literary translation.[4] The idea behind this and a couple of similar papers around this time was that translating literary works could be as enjoyable as writing fiction, poetry, or essays; in addition, this pleasure could be enhanced for both readers and translators by the strategic use of appropriate illustrations.

***

Before taking his long-service leave, Lawrence Wong had invited me to talk to his students about my translation experiences. Having previously sketched out some ideas at a seminar in Edinburgh, I now prepared a more formal version, although it was unsettling to discover that my activities in the 1980s by 2006 had become a matter of history. Because there proved to be an audience for it, I continued to work on these topics, speaking at guest lectures and conferences in Hong Kong, Macao, the US, New Zealand, and China over the next few years.

The two papers I'd exposed to student and public audiences had undergone much revision from their audiences, both captive and voluntary; and I began to see other issues evolving. I now decided to explore these translation experiences more systematically, moving further away from research on modern Chinese literature and toward research on modern Chinese literary translation. Once I was at the City University of Hong Kong, it was time to convert these experiences into a book-length manuscript. Thanks to Zhang Longxi, City University provided me with the facilities and encouragement that enabled me to work long hours without interruption. Anders had moved to the Macau Ricci Institute as publications editor but returned at weekends so I could consult him. In the end, *Translation Zones in Modern China* almost wrote itself.

Translation Zones was my attempt to synthesize two very different translation experiences in China within a theoretical frame: it gave me a great deal of pleasure and certainly increased my confidence in translating and teaching translation. It was duly published in 2011. The main response has been from Chinese students, who have politely requested written interviews. COVID-19 of course put an end to visits to China between 2019 and 2022, but the emails kept coming.

***

Hong Kong had given a huge welcome to two of my main translatees: Bei Dao and Chen Kaige. I no longer translated work by these two (plenty of people were now engaged in doing so); instead, in October 2006, I proposed setting up a Bei Dao archive at the CUHK library. The core of the archive would initially consist of a substantial deposit of original manuscripts of poems given or addressed to me. Bei Dao, then a resident in the US, had visited CUHK on several occasions, most recently in the summer of 2006 as a visiting scholar in the translation department. As well as teaching a course in Chinese literature, he gave an immensely successful poetry reading in June 2006 with me (see chapter 9). CUHK was also one of the first places in the world to recognize his talent. His works were first published in Chinese and in English translation by *Renditions* and by The Chinese University Press. In some cases, these were the first published versions of the originals. The CUHK library also possessed many of his published works, mostly housed in the Chinese-language Ch'ien Mu Library at New Asia College. Finally, Bei Dao and his heirs were to exercise copyright over the materials in the archive in accordance with Hong Kong law.

By placing these materials in the context of the author's life and contemporary debates, the archive was planned to draw attention to the fundamental dilemmas of modern Chinese writers in reconciling the demands of political concerns, literary professionals, and domestic life. The collection was formally opened by Dr. Colin Storey, the head librarian, in March 2009; crucial support from Leo Ma, the head of the New Asia College Chi'en Mu Library, included establishing a home for the material. In 2010 the archive was reorganized: it is now located in the main library (under the unfortunate change of name to "Bonnie S. McDougall Collection on Bei Dao") and is accompanied by works by other modern Chinese writers with whom I don't claim a close relationship. The recently retired head librarian, Louise Jones, should be warmly thanked for having arranged for the digitization of the collection, which remains a part of the university library. I am currently preparing a similar collection of archival material relating to Chen Kaige.

**

Another step, starting around 2005–2006, was to engage finally with Chinese women writers. While working at the FLP, I had translated poetry by a small group of new women writers for *Chinese Literature*, but because I was commissioned, I can't claim any credit for choosing to translate them. I was not encouraged either by the poor reception to my 1992 translation of Wang Anyi's novella *Brocade Valley*. Then, after I'd moved to Hong Kong, I consulted Wong Nim Yan about local women poets. Among them was Ng Mei-kwan, although it wasn't until after my return to Sydney in 2010 that I began work in earnest on translating her poems.

One effort that ended in disappointment was my request to translate a novel by Lily Lee (a.k.a Lillian Lee, Lilian Lee, and Li Bik-wah). In the end, her publishers turned me down, and as far as I know the book that had formed the basis for Chen Kaige's *Farewell My Concubine* remains untranslated. In the end, it was a completely different Hong Kong writer whose work dominated my translating and research over the last decade.

***

In 2008, I took part in the first Sino-British Literary Translation workshop, a brave experiment in training Chinese-to-English and English-to-Chinese literary translation. On the British side, a group of juniors mainly from the UK were recruited, whereas on the Chinese side the participants were mainly literary editors and translators. I didn't keep notes of this occasion, but I remember with mixed feelings the rustic conditions on top of Moganshan in a remote corner of Zhejiang. The event was regarded as successful by its sponsors, and a second meeting took place in Suzhou the following year, this time sponsored on the British side by the Penguin Publishing Group with the support of Arts Council England.

As described in a short article I wrote for the British Centre for Literary Translation, the Suzhou event was marked by a great goodwill shown by all parties, enlivened by informal visits to the old city's cafes and bars in the evenings.[5] The author of our group's assignment was Sheng Keyi, a younger writer who had recently achieved fame with her bleakly realistic portraits of love and sex in China in the early Xi Jinping years. My group was a little worried that at my advanced age I wouldn't know (or wish to know) the vocabulary of sexual liberation, but after the first session we began to be more informal, reaching the sensible decision, for instance, that expressions such as "fuck-buddy," "courtesy screw," and "friends with benefits" could be used variously according to context. Translation can be a dirty business. It could also get rowdy: on one occasion a frustrated member of the group left a discussion in rage.

Finding sponsors for these events had been a problem, but finally a third round, now called a Chinese-English Literary Translation Course, was held in Huangshan, Anhui, in 2014. At first, I was excited by the prospect of a visit to one of China's most famous mountains, where I'd not been before, but it turned out that the mountain itself was some distance away. This, the last workshop I took part in, was altogether larger and more elaborate. Anders, who came along as well, was recruited to carry out some editing for a Beijing state publisher. For me, the highlight of the events was when Beijing-based award-winning author and president of the China Writers Association Tie Ning attended several of our group's sessions, and I relished the role of interpreting between her and the young translators.

Overall, I was impressed by the obvious benefits of group collaborative efforts in literary translation. As our impassioned participants strode up and down the room, sometimes shouting to make themselves heard above competing voices, it was clear that literary translating was no simple matter but a deeply involved personal commitment. Especially in the last two workshops, I became convinced that group translation could, in some ways and in some cases, create an environment ripe for spirited, engaging translation.

Notes

1. The Research Centre for Translation had been established as a research unit in 1971 as part of the Institute of Chinese Studies at CUHK.
2. Dung Kai-cheung, "Spring Garden Lane," 111–113; as noted later, this is a chapter in one of Dung Kai-cheung's novels. "Spring Garden Lane" initially seemed to me to be an independent piece of writing (i.e., an "essay"). It was only later that I found out that it is in fact a chapter in a work of fiction.
3. Ding Xilin's "Dear Husband" (co-translated with Flora Lam) and Leung Ping-kwan's "Beijing Sketches" are both in *Renditions* 69, Spring 2008.
4. McDougall, "Literary Translation: The Pleasure Principle." The article is based on unpublished talks.
5. McDougall, "CELT 09: The Suzhou Experience," 50–52.

CHAPTER 13

WRITERS IN THREE PLACES

In spring 2009, as our time at CUHK came to an end, I left Hong Kong for a month-long visit to Australia. Anders and I then met up in New Zealand where we embarked on a two-month academic visit, promoting the power and the glory that is translation studies. We then returned to Hong Kong where I took up my one-year position at City University. In August 2010, I returned to live in Sydney, about thirty-five years since I'd departed for the US, while Anders continued his position as editor at the Macau Ricci Institute before joining me and our son in Sydney in 2012. Thanks to Wang Yiyan, the head of the Chinese studies department at the University of Sydney, I resumed teaching. I'm still here in Sydney with a university office, having been granted different titles throughout the years, continuing research and translation, but since 2017 I'm no longer teaching.

***

Around 2012, I was invited by Josh Stenberg, then a graduate student in Canada, to contribute a story in an anthology of modern Chinese fiction that he was editing in collaboration with the Chinese Writers

Association. From among a list of possible writers and works, I chose without hesitation the story "Irina's Hat" by Tie Ning.

I'd first heard about Tie Ning around 1982 from Bei Dao, who had selected one of her stories for translation into Esperanto when he was an editor at the FLP; he was one of many who praised her persuasive short stories in the early 1980s. In 2006 she had quite amazingly been appointed head of the Chinese Writers Association, after its first and only other head, Ba Jin, had stepped down. For a woman to succeed in this high post was startling enough, but having the head of this organization also being relatively young and associated with liberal values in literature seemed to promise an open future for writers. We met again at the translation workshop in 2014 and then again when she headed a delegation that visited Sydney in 2015. Her visit to Australia was at a time when the two countries were on reasonably good terms and such visits were common. It was such a pleasure to meet again, I felt, as she gave me a warm hug.

The other reason for choosing this story was that it seemed to be suitable teaching material for my translation class at the University of Sydney, consisting of a group of eight Chinese students from the mainland plus one from Sydney. The plan was that our group would translate the story and oversee its progress after returning it to the editor, staying in touch throughout the rest of the publication progress. Each student was listed as one of the story's translators, and each was issued a copy of the volume when it was published plus a share of the translation fee.

You can be sure that heated debates took place among the students as the translation took shape. Still, despite there being many (sometimes conflicting) voices in the class, a general unity was achieved as students read their version of the story aloud and, after a brief pause, welcomed views from the rest of the class. One issue on which we reached general agreement was about sex. As was common enough in those years, the storyline showed sympathy for the extramarital sexual conduct of the two main characters, but the treatment of the gay couple included disparaging remarks from the narrator (that is, likely to be echoing the author's own view) about their clothing and their furtive recourse to the airline's lavatory. There was nothing we could do about this. Nonetheless, we were gratified when we discovered on publication that our story had been chosen for the book title.[1] Tie Ning would also have been pleased.

During the editing phase, Josh Stenberg and I had some exchanges about the use of "like" as a conjunction and finally agreed that "as though" could be interchanged with "as if." I knew that "like" as a conjunction had appeared as early as the 1940s, as for instance in dialogue by crime writer Raymond Chandler (1888–1959), and had no trouble with that: it was only in its use in the authorial voice that I found objectionable. I now concede that "like" is commonly used as a subordinate conjunction in the authorial voice in English-language fiction but still abstain from using it myself in speech or writing.

I've now come to realize that I'm a relic of the past in this regard, as no doubt in many others. It's left me with the uneasy sense that I'm no longer able to address in contemporary idiom an American or British readership, and despite now living in Australia, I believe that my command of spoken Australian English has also slipped. One possible reason for this could be that I'd lived too long abroad in countries where my native language was either remote from the language of that country (China and Norway) or else dangerously close (the US and the UK). Or maybe it's just that I've grown old. In consequence, at the very least, I thought that I should probably withdraw from any kind of translation that requires fluency in colloquial or everyday speech. Just when I was starting to feel confident about translating, I found myself embarking on new projects that would push me to the limits of my abilities.

***

Not long before I left Hong Kong in 2010, I was introduced by Wong Nim Yan to the poetry of Ng Mei-kwan, one of a small group of women poets who were becoming known for their distinctive focus on interior sensitivities. The following year, when my teaching duties at the University of Sydney were still light, I returned to translating Ng Mei-kwan's poems. Although it was some time before we met in person, we produced between us a series of poems for which we sought publication. In a way, translating these poems reminded me of earlier efforts in translating shadows poetry, in which explosive sentiments were expressed obliquely. Among Ng Mei-kwan's work, however, one poem stood out: the overtly political "Rainstorm" ("Juyu" 巨雨), its title referring to the May 1989 massacres in China's major cities, including Beijing and Shanghai. During a visit to Sydney in 2011, Ng Mei-kwan attended a poetry recital sponsored by *Southerly*, one of Australia's leading literary journals, where she read this poem aloud in Chinese, and I followed with our English translation. This poem was then included on the journal's website *The Long Paddock*. The remainder of the poems that I translated with her assistance have been published in the Hong Kong online journal *Cha*.

***

Another new venture was easier, if only because I had advice from two experts. When I had been a staff member at Harvard in the late 1970s, I'd had free access to various courses, and I've never regretted choosing a two-semester course in Old Norse. By then my French, German, and Latin had been to some extent replaced by Chinese and Japanese, and it felt good to switch back to European languages. I've never become very fluent in modern Swedish, however, despite regular visits to Stockholm. That didn't stop our close friend Torbjörn Lodén, retired professor of Chinese at the University of Stockholm, from approaching me in 2019 about translating a short brochure for tourists about the tiny village of Ventlinge, on the southern Swedish island of Öland. Torbjörn and his wife Lena Jönsson had a farmhouse there which was formerly the home of the poet Anna Rydstedt (1928–1994). The brochure produced by Torbjörn, Lena, and other people of the area was of course in Swedish, and because my grasp of Swedish was not particularly firm, Anders soon emerged as the dominant partner in our translation. Translating the brochure itself was not difficult: although we lacked necessary local knowledge, help was nearby. There were several poems in this brochure, and in the end Anders and I translated them as well as the rest of the text; eventually we translated another batch of poems unrelated to the brochure. That same year, following a conference hosted by Torbjörn in Stockholm, Anders and I spent a few days with them in Anna Rydstedt's old home. Most recently, my sister-in-law and I have finished a translation of a 1940s Swedish crime novel by a famous woman writer, and we are hoping to attract the attention of a British publisher.

***

These three women writers (Tie Ning, Ng Mei-kwan, and Anna Rydstedt) represented a new role for me in translation: unlike with my earlier translatees (including He Qifang, Mao Zedong, Lu Xun, Xu Guangping, Bei Dao, and Ah Cheng), I was no longer under an obligation to arrange publishers and publication, protection and publicity: the writers could do this, with their better knowledge and wider experience. No more glossaries, no more earnest explications; my job was only to translate. If I missed the sense of urgency, I welcomed the relief that followed. As it turned out, it wasn't going to be that easy.

Notes

1. Josh Stenberg, ed., *Irina's Hat: New Short Stories from China* (Portland, ME: Merwin Asia, 2013).

CHAPTER 14

FROM *ATLAS* TO LOVE STORIES TO *CATALOG* TO LOCKDOWNS

Alongside *Letters between Two*, the most complex translation process in which I've ever taken part is *Atlas: The Archaeology of an Imaginary City* (*Dituji* 地圖集)[1] by Dung Kai-cheung, co-translated with the author and Anders and published by Columbia University Press in 2012. The story of this undertaking began around 2007, as I was searching for translation material for my classes at CUHK. It was my dear friend Wong Nim Yan to whom I'd turned to learn about Hong Kong writers, and in a further discussion over lunch among the three of us (Dung Kai-cheung, Anders, and me), Dung Kai-cheung mentioned his novel *Atlas*. Later, with the author's guidance, I chose the chapters "Spring Garden Lane" and "Ice House Street" ("Xuechangjie" 雪廠街) as ideal class exercises as well as material for *Renditions*; later, teaching at City University in 2009, I added "Sugar Street" ("Tangjie" 糖街) to send to the magazine *Edinburgh Review*, which had requested fiction from Hong Kong. Ever since I've worked with him, I've considered Dung Kai-cheung to be one of the most creative and original writers I've known.

I was so impressed by the stories in *Atlas* that I soon became seized by the idea of translating the whole book.[2] On discovering that it was more complex than I'd thought from those three chapters, I slowly became aware that it wasn't going to be easy. In the end, I persuaded the author and Anders to collaborate with me in an elaborate procedure whereby we divided the four parts of the book among us: each would make an initial draft for subsequent revision by one of the other two, and at the end of this process, we would all would read the entire manuscript. We also created a working glossary to which each of us contributed individual words and phrases as well as references to books, institutions, and other phenomena.

We brought our own particular skills to this exercise. The author had the best understanding of Hong Kong, Cantonese, and Mandarin, and (naturally) his own work; I was the only native English speaker and the most familiar with Chinese-to-English literary translation; and Anders was a historian of traditional China, fluent in both Chinese and English and deeply engaged in Hong Kong history and popular culture. For most of the time during which our cooperation was active, we were all living in Hong Kong or Macao, so contact was relatively easy. The whole translation process reached a climactic end in a Shatin coffee shop that kindly allowed us to debate our last remaining issues for about three hours. It is now virtually impossible to distinguish which words, phrases, or paragraphs in the translation came from which of the three co-translators.

As publication approached, we were now living in three different places: Hong Kong, Macao, and Sydney. Each of us also had concurrent projects to attend to, and it was several years before we were able to send a final manuscript to a publisher. David Der-wei Wang extended invaluable assistance in providing a pathway to Columbia University Press. Once the contract was signed, the author wrote a preface, and I contributed an introduction; acknowledgements and brief notes on the translators then followed the main text. The post-publication reviews were excellent, and

From *Atlas* to Love Stories to *Catalog* to Lockdowns   189

the book became part of the curriculum for several university Chinese departments. Both the Chinese and the English versions are still in print, and at least one other translation is based on ours.

The true complexity in this project was, of course, the manuscript itself. Each of the four sections has its own significance and a style to match. *Atlas* is an extraordinary assemblage of fact and fiction; of history, geography, philosophy, and politics; of imagination and wit; and of realistic anecdotes and fantasy. It is a novel without a plot; it covers a wide range of characters of whom none is dominant; and acts of sex and violence are implied. The profusion of place names in the early chapters is daunting, as are the abstract conceptualizations toward the end. Still, throughout, the author's strange blend of humor and distress infuses the apparent detachment he brings to re-creating his city's past and present, just as his archaeologist of the future in the book attempts to re-create it through old maps, blueprints, and urban planning.

I'd started this book by reading the lively short anecdotes of individual lives in Hong Kong; moving to the beginning, which was very different, I felt stranded. Most of parts 1 and 2 seemed almost impenetrable even when I could actually understand them. In the two or three years as I read the whole text again and again, I finally began to blend the different shades of meaning from chapter to chapter, so that even the more obscure passages moved from being a mixture of pleasure and bafflement to yielding a more comprehensive grasp of different sorts of meaning. A lot of it I still find baffling, but the pleasure, and even the fun of it, have thankfully become clearer.

Sales figures for Columbia University Press for *Atlas* were not impressive, however: 770 copies were sold in 2012; in 2016, this number shrank to 99. I expect we get royalties, but Anders now handles these things.

***

The process of translation with *Atlas* was complicated (although never messy), and its reception was encouraging. Our undertaking to translate

Meng hua lu 夢華錄, a later work by Dung Kai-cheung also called *The Catalog*, seemed simpler because there would be only two translators, Anders and I, plus the author as advisor. It also turned out that that we would in the end have the same publisher, Columbia University Press.

The title *Meng hua lu* is derived from that of a book from the early Southern Song dynasty (1127–1279), *Dongjing meng hua lu* 東京夢華錄, or *Dreams of the Splendors of the Eastern Capital*, by Meng Yuanlao. It is a nostalgic description of a former capital city lost to invaders from the north.

Unlike *Atlas*, there were complications regarding the text itself. The book is a collection of ninety-nine brief narratives of life in Hong Kong in the late 1990s. It first appeared in 1999 in Hong Kong, with the author's name given as Kai and the title appearing in English only as *The Catalog*. This original Hong Kong edition was published by Trio Publication.

On subsequent publication in Taipei, however, it was just called *Meng hua lu* on the title page, as well as on the front cover, the English title appearing only as supplementary on the front cover , and also on a paper sleeve wrapped around the cover.

When arrangements for publication of our complete English translation were finally settled some ten years later in 2021, Dung Kai-cheung chose a new title: *A Catalog of Such Stuff as Dreams are Made On*. It's likely that the appearance of the book was delayed by the pandemic that swept through the world, but there were other factors.

This translation began as classroom teaching material at the University of Sydney with up to a dozen students at a time taking part. With *Atlas* in the hands of the publishers, I selected for teaching material a few of the stories from *Catalog*. The class, composed of a dozen or so Chinese-speaking undergraduates, at first found the mix of realistic and fantastic details hard to follow, and because I was also uncertain, I appealed to the author for help and sought assistance from Anders. I think we came

From *Atlas* to Love Stories to *Catalog* to Lockdowns

up with decent translations, and so I continued translating more of the sketches largely for my own enjoyment.

As we proceeded at our leisure through *Catalog*, an opportunity for immediate publication suddenly appeared: the Penguin Publishing Group decided to run a special series of very short books on Hong Kong to mark the twentieth anniversary of retrocession in 1997, and Dung Kai-cheung, as one of the now former colony's most original writers, was invited to contribute. With help from Dung Kai-cheung, who selected twenty-five chapters (or sketches) out of those we had already translated, Anders and I produced a slender book with a completely new title provided by the author: *Cantonese Love Stories: Twenty-five Vignettes of a City*. It was published as a Penguin Special in Sydney in 2017. The contents included a brief "Translators' Note" by Anders and me and a much longer introductory essay, "Dream of a Dream: On Language, Love and Storytelling" by a "Virginia Anderson," dated March 2106. (A percipient reader might perceive that the latter was written by the author himself.) Penguin offered Anders and me a flat fee for our translation, but I'm afraid I have no idea how much it was or in what currency we received it.

We three were pleased and relieved when *Cantonese Love Stories* was published. On our visits to Hong Kong over the next couple of years, we saw it prominently featured in the local English-language bookshops. Turning to the complete text was the obvious next step, so with the generous assistance of the author, Anders and I completed the translation of *Catalog*, including the *Cantonese Love Stories* sketches with some minor changes and under the new title. We submitted it to Columbia University Press in 2018. For complicated reasons, including copyright issues and the pandemic lockdowns, publication was delayed, but the book was published in 2022.

***

Like *Atlas*, *Catalog* defies conventional classification: there are no central characters, no sequential narrative from chapter to chapter, and no identifiable authorial voice. In contrast to *Atlas*, however, the stories deal with the everyday life of ordinary people in contemporary Hong Kong. In this work, Dung Kai-cheung transforms Hong Kong's obsessions with consumer products into strange and often fantastic narratives. The author's predilection for playfulness blended with a serious undertone is also a notable characteristic of many of these sketches.

When Dung Kai-cheung originally selected for *Catalog* the electronic devices, foodstuffs, fashionable clothing, shoes, and accessories he saw around him, he had chosen them more or less at random. After the passage of more than a decade, he became more aware of what he calls "a touch of darkness" in the sketches, although he claimed that the individual storylines are not deliberately weird but on the contrary are based on everyday existence. Many of the stories come close to not having an ending; few offer an opening to the future. Finally, addressing his Taiwan readers, Dung Kai-cheung assured them that his occasional use of Cantonese in dialogue should not deter them from engaging with his book. As he noted, language is a site of multiple meanings, and the reader can infer what is meant or referenced from the story overall. (This assurance is not necessarily valid for readers whose native language is not any form of Chinese.)

The language used in *Catalog* is complex, including more Cantonese expressions than in *Atlas*, for instance. In other respects, the two works are similar. The narrative language is still differentiated from the dialogue: for example, there are more function words in the dialogue, such as pronouns and final particles. Children and the less educated, unsurprisingly, tend to speak in colloquial Cantonese; dialogue by young, educated women and men (especially university students) is more likely to adopt Mandarin vocabulary and grammar Passages of written description are predominantly in Mandarin, being perhaps an accurate depiction of writing styles in Hong Kong in the late 1990s. The spoken language is occasionally vulgar (e.g., in "The Cowboy Hat") but never obscene.

From *Atlas* to Love Stories to *Catalog* to Lockdowns 193

In its cast of characters, *Catalog* is singularly homogeneous. In the majority of the sketches, the central character is a young, educated, urban female: schoolgirls, teenagers, university students, and office ladies, who often act on impulse with occasionally tragic results. The young men feature for the most part as the other half of a couple: they tend to be reactive, sometimes violent, often baffled by their partner's behavior. Most female-male relationships involve sexual encounters that are sometimes satisfactory, sometimes not.

Absences are significant: there is just one character of European descent, a Mormon, presumably from the US, who speaks with a heavy accent, and a single mainlander, a young man now settled in Hong Kong; there are no Filipina "helpers," Indian tailors, or other ethnic minorities. Government authorities are also absent: there are no politicians or bureaucrats, only a single social worker and few (mostly passive or neutral) police. There is space for the socially marginalized as well as mothers and (less often) fathers typically in secondary roles, but the rich (except for a bumptious young man with a taste for expensive watches) do not appear, nor do farmers or others based in the New Territories countryside; a small number of central characters live in or visit the Outlying Islands. Only the bumptious young man mentioned previously drives a car; bicycles and motorcycles make appearances, but most of the characters commute on public transport and live and work in an urban environment. The locations are sometimes but not always specified, and the intended readership would be able to identify them. There is no past in these stories, only the present.

On the whole, the characters in *Catalog* do not resemble the academic teachers and students or literary professionals among whom the author now spends most of his life, and the relatively few intellectuals or university students in male roles are not particularly likable. It is Dung Kai-cheung's memories of his family, friends, and neighbors that would have prepared him for these later encounters in the streets, shopping malls, street food stalls, and tea restaurants. The depiction of young women is particularly impressive: there is no condescension in his accounts of their apparent eccentricities, only cool observation infused with sympathy.

Perhaps it is these characters' highly circumscribed lives that leave them vulnerable. Their possessions become their obsessions, enabling them to protect themselves and to cope with undefined hostile forces from outside. The young women are often strategically clever, whether through instinct or calculation: they find solutions for breaking free from their restraints by altering their behavior, which may include apparently trivial acts such as changing their phone company. Not all of the stories have a happy ending: for many characters, death is the only thing that releases them from their troubles. For the most part, however, the stories are about private, personal, and individual survival in an anonymous, unresponsive, and possibly threatening society.

Notes

1. *Atlas* was first published in 1997 by Lianhe chubanshe in Taibei. It has the title *Dituji* 地圖集 on the title page. The front cover had a longer title in both Chinese and English: *Dituji: Yi ge xiangxiang de dechengshi de kaoguxue* 地圖集：一個想像的城市的考古學 and *Atlas: The Archaeology of an Imaginary City*. A second edition was published in Taibei in 2011 by Linking Books.
2. A diligent and thoughtful essay by Uganda Sze Pui Kwan, "Strategizing Hong Kong Literature in the world," compares the author's initial translation of *Atlas* and the later version. Although familiar with the first attempt, Kwan is not wholly accurate in describing the process that culminated in the second publication; for instance, it was on my initiative that we formed our gang of three, rather than anyone else's.

Part VI

Afterthoughts

Chapter 15

Translation Transactions

In the words of the brilliant but self-destructive novelist X. Trapnel, "biography and memoirs can never be true, since they can't include every conceivable circumstance of what happened."[1] If so, this chapter may be the book's most unreliable. After I entered into direct contact with living authors, I began to find translation increasing in importance and then taking over my life. I continued to write on topics other than translation, but they don't appear in this book.

Although Chinese-to-English translation of modern literature looks as if it's a narrow field, I certainly don't think it's easy to build a reputation for accurate and readable work. For me, as I've mentioned previously, translation was at first a kind of substantiation of research that I'd enjoyed doing and imagined that the reader might also enjoy. Only gradually, after I'd translated work by authors I knew personally, did I become aware that translation itself involved many issues I was barely conscious of. Later, I have summarized some of the articles I've written since then on the nature of literary translation to relate experiences that made me aware of the independent status of literary translation, with or without personal contact.

In my first publishable translations, direct transactions with Chinese writers and publishers were unthinkable: He Qifang was alive but out of reach, and he died the year after my study of his work was published. Even the authors of some of the newer work appearing in China in the late 1970s were still remote figures with whom I had no means of contact, and I scarcely even wondered what if any problem or advantage should arise from any such efforts. It was only when I moved to China and entered the world of Chinese writing that direct transactions with authors and often publishers became not only possible but advisable. In retrospect, I have wondered if my upbringing in a semi-secret organization had led to excessive secrecy about my translatees in order to protect them from official attention in my academic studies. Interestingly, Anders was initially more sensitive than I about the need for discretion.

This account has several gaps. My lightweight portable typewriter accompanied me around the world until we moved to Oslo, when computers increasingly became the only instrument of record. (I recall traveling to Cambridge, Massachusetts, with the typewriter in a rucksack on my back; I left it there.) Some operations were still primitive, however. Moving to Hong Kong in 2006, where I had to switch between two offices as well as my local residence, I repeatedly lost material including not only correspondence but translation drafts and commentaries during my five years there. Back now in Sydney, it's easier to keep records, thanks to the University of Sydney and to my son, now a professional computer expert. Readers may be grateful that little remains of my typewritten or early computer-based correspondence and drafts.

***

There was a time during my early years as a student in high school and university when I saw philosophy as the guide to finding meaning in life and learning. I wasn't very good at it, and eventually I drifted away. Time passed, again, and I returned to my first and true love: words and reading, literature and language. I began to play with concepts, definitions, and other delightful tricks with language and meaning. Even as translation occupied more and more of my time, old habits persisted, however, and translation itself only gradually became a subject for research.

My first amateurish efforts, in talks given in 1987, 1989, and 1994 on literary translation, remain unpublished. The first published effort appeared under the clumsy title "Problems and Possibilities in Translating Contemporary Chinese Literature."[2] It contains my accounts of translating poetry by Bei Dao and Qiu Xiaolong; short fiction by Bei Dao, Chen Maiping, Chen Kaige, and Ah Cheng; the play *If I Were Real* (*Jiaru wo shi zhen de* 假如我是真的) by Sha Yexin and others; and the scripts of two films directed by Chen Kaige. The main drift was to claim "that contrary to conventional belief, translating poetry may be a less troublesome task than translating fiction, drama and film; that the needs and pleasures of different kinds of readers and audiences can and should be taken into account; and that we should press as hard as possible for control of the final versions of our efforts." For this I drew on comments on translating the items listed previously in their respective chapters.

It was when I spent two months at CUHK in 2005 that I suddenly found myself being expected to take seriously phenomena that I'd previously underrated. What made it easy to comply was that my so-called research went little further than autobiography, with only cursory treatment being given to abstract theories. (The titles sounded good, though.)[3] Even then, I didn't see any issue that persuaded me to pay attention to translation theories. It was only exposure over the next few years that led to better understanding of what I'd been doing as a secondary occupation. Leaving Edinburgh and not caring to stay longer in the UK, I was finding Hong Kong to be an ideal place for the next five years and literary translation the ideal occupation, both for practice and for discussion.

The first translation conference I'd attended was at Hong Kong University in the late 1960s. All I recall now are the bad-tempered retorts of translators hotly rejecting any criticism received and the equally keen pleasure taken by others criticizing someone else's translation. Returning to Hong Kong in 2006 to teach at the CUHK's translation department was entering a new world, encouraging me to speculate more about the wider realms of translation. Then, becoming the acting director of the Research Centre for Translation at the Institute of Chinese Studies increased a sense of pressure to keep up with this world. Still amateurish, however, were the three talks I gave on what was a kind of joke I invented against myself: the pleasure principle. The first talk, given in 2007, was followed with further talks on the idea in 2008 and 2009.[4] All this concept meant was that just as we read the literature of our own country or in our own native language because it's a pleasure, producing a translation of a literary work of another country or native language should be (and perhaps should be even more) a pleasure for both translator and reader.

Only the first of these three talks has been published.[5] The concept of translation as a pleasure, although not a new proposition in translation studies,[6] had not previously been raised with reference to contemporary Chinese literary studies, so it generated some attention. One of its main propositions describes the situation in which specialist Chinese translators (who translated from Chinese into English) in China were senior Chinese professionals who knew the target readership, through their own reading and experience, better than the political management who dictated their duties. In another article, I also point out the importance of illustration in literary translation, which has generally been ignored as an aspect of Chinese translation studies. Possibly because I wasn't very familiar with translation theory, I dwelt on the matter of illustration for several years.

In 1995 I wrote a short article under the title "Chinese Errors and English Infelicities" for publication in a British journal that promptly expired. Because it contained an unusually harsh review of a translation by a well-known scholar, it was probably just as well. A happier occasion was in 1998 when I was contacted by the noted translation scholar Peter Bush, the director of the British Centre of Literary Translation, to correct an item for publication on Chinese literary translation. I was also invited to give a research seminar there later that year. I assume this happened but lack records to confirm it.

***

One of the pleasures of living in Hong Kong was easy access to Australia, where I still had family and friends. On a visit in August 2007, I gave a paper at the University of Sydney called "Why Cut the Pirate's Poem? (& Five Good Reasons for Reading Hong Kong Literature)." The third and last of the *Pirates of the Caribbean* films had just been released, with Chow Yun-fat in the role of Captain Sao Feng, Pirate Lord of the South China Sea. With a production budget of nearly US$300 million, the film was claimed at the time of production to be the most expensive film ever made. Intrigued, I made an aspect of this event a starting point for an informal oral presentation to old friends and colleagues:

> There was something of a stir in Hong Kong recently when it became known that the Chinese release of *Pirates of the Caribbean: At World's End* had cut in half the screen appearance of one of Hong Kong's favorite actors, Chow Yun Fat. The censorship board did not permit, for instance, the Chinese pirate to identify himself as having come from Singapore, although the omission of this scene made nonsense of the story line. Another cut was Chow Yun Fat reciting a poem by Li Bai: the problem could not have been the poem itself, so that the only reason for censoring it had to be because Chow read it aloud in Cantonese.[7]

From a literary perspective, Cantonese is preferable to Mandarin (i.e., Putonghua, Modern Standard Chinese) as the language in which to read the poem because modern spoken Cantonese is closer to Tang Chinese than Mandarin, and the rhymes actually do rhyme in Cantonese.[8] This pleasure is denied to mainland audiences, where the specter of any kind of separatism, even linguistic, is deeply offensive to the authorities.[9]

The talk I gave to a student audience on a 2009 visit to Sydney, this time on the theme of illustration, listed examples of the strategic use of illustration in translating Hong Kong poetry: four poems by Leung Bing-kwan, written during his visit to Beijing in 2002, and two poems, "Rainstorm" and "Hermeneutics" ("Jieshixue" 解釋學) by Ng Mei-kwan, written slightly later. My translations of these poems were distributed at the outset to the audience, which consisted mainly of Chinese students at Western Sydney University; they responded enthusiastically to these poems, immediately grasping their underlying significance. These talks have never been published, although I still regard them as among my best.

***

My 2011 *Translation Zones in Modern China*, which was mostly written in Hong Kong, was more descriptive than analytic, apart from the chapter on power relations affecting translators. There were, nevertheless, still several aspects that bothered me. I grew up in the Australian "cultural cringe"[10] era of the 1950s and 1960s, so I strove to make my written English as close to the Queen's English as it could be. This tendency was strengthened during brief visits to the US in the 1960s, reinforced during the year I spent in London in 1975, and became even more pronounced when I lived in Cambridge, Massachusetts, from 1976 to 1980, where an Australian accent was pretty much unknown: Ross Terrill, from Melbourne, and Patrick Dewes Hanan, from New Zealand, were the only two scholars in East Asian studies from my part of the world. From there I went to Beijing, where my spoken English was occasionally incomprehensible to both native and foreign interlocutors, and it was by no means corrected during a further four years in Oslo.

Part of the reason for moving to Edinburgh at the end of 1980s was to live in an English-speaking country, and Scotland was more beckoning than England, given my father's origins in Glasgow. Still, my Australian accent would be ridiculed during visits to southern England, although my written English possibly improved during my time there. Returning to Hong Kong in 2006, I found an Australian voice was possibly more common in my university-based social life there than any of the UK or US versions. By that time, I was already preparing, somewhat haphazardly, for a return to my homeland.

Before doing so, I spent time with a small number of Hong Kong writers, most prominent of whom was Dung Kai-cheung. Mainland China had become an increasingly divided place since 2006: the government seemed to be moving from harsh measures to harsher ones and then back to less harsh ones, whereas writers and academics still seemed, for the most part, protected. Although I avoided translating mainland writers, a policy to which I was now firmly committed, I was accepting invitations to give lectures or papers at prominent mainland universities. Finally, a long visit to New Zealand allowed me for the first time to assert quite vehemently to broader and more senior audiences the core value of translation, proclaiming to all who would listen the forthcoming dominance of translation (including literary translation) around the world.

***

Thanks to good friends and colleagues, in 2010 I became affiliated with the Chinese studies department at the University of Sydney, where I bravely undertook teaching classes on translation to students from China, Hong Kong, Taiwan, and Australia: almost all were ethnic Chinese, but some students' knowledge of written Chinese and Chinese literature was relatively poor, whereas others were more sophisticated and could understand complex literary issues. In this context, Dung Kai-cheung's sometimes bizarre stories shook the self-confidence of even the better students. In the meantime, my *Translation Zones* book appeared, encouraging me to pontificate again on translation issues.

Further bolstering my self-confidence over the next few years were invitations to take part in two Harvard-based projects. The first offer was from David Der-wei Wang in 2012 to contribute to his massive project *A New Literary History of Modern China*; with over a thousand pages and 140 contributors, it took five years to reach readers. I chose for my contribution to compare three novels in which an element of fantasy was dominant. The earliest was the novel *Yanzhi kou* 胭脂扣 (Rouge) by Lilian Lee, an excerpt from which I'd chosen as a classroom text in my CUHK teaching. The 1988 film, based on the book, starring Anita Mui and Leslie Cheung, had been a huge hit in East Asia, although it had little impact on other readers beyond its implied references to the recently signed agreement between China and the UK on Hong Kong's retrocession in 1997. I remain disappointed that the publisher turned down my request to translate the novel, which as far as I can tell has not yet been translated. It was some consolation that I'd been given this opportunity to write about it. Another reason for my interest in Lee was that another of her novels provided the plot of Chen Kaige's second-most famous film, *Farewell My Concubine* (see chapter 8).

The next item was Dung Kai-cheng's *Atlas*, which I'd co-translated with the author and Anders (see chapter 14). The third was Wong Bik Wan's *Doomsday Hotel* (*Mori jiudian* 末日酒店), published as a bilingual text; again, it was a work that I'd heard much about and wished I'd been asked to translate because it features a beautifully fantasized version of Macao's famous Bela Vista Hotel, where we'd stayed several times. A final comment: the title of my essay, "Hong Kong's Literary Retrocession in Three Fantastical Novels," was not the one I originally offered: I would never use the word "fantastical."

A few years later, I was invited to contribute to a new collection of translations of Lu Xun's essays, edited by Eileen J. Cheng and Kirk A. Denton. Although I was still prejudiced against this literary hero for his patronizing attitude toward Xu Guangping, I was equally prejudiced in his favor as a writer.[11]

***

In 2016–2017, an exercise in comparative translation that I very much enjoyed was a contribution to *Into English: Poems, Translations, Commentaries*, edited by Martha Collins and Kevin Prufer and published in 2017.[12] It compares three translations of one of modern China's best-loved poems,

Xu Zhimo's "Second Farewell to Cambridge"; the translators were: Kai-yu Hsu (whose translation is from 1963), Michelle Yeh (1992), and Hugh Grigg (2012). I had never formally translated this poem myself but had often taught it because it naturally suited all kinds of classes and students. The timespan of almost fifty years covered by these three translators was almost irrelevant, even including Grigg's choice of publication online. There were nevertheless several points of difference and similarity. In the end, although the other two translation are graceful and sensitive, it seemed to me that only Hsu caught the significance of the final stanza: "I shake my sleeves a little / Not to bring away a patch of cloud." To "shake his sleeve," much as a Peking Opera performer would do, indicates that the speaker pauses to recover his poise and come to a decision, painfully resolving to leave this place that he loves so deeply while being unable to take any of its beauty with him. It's a decision that many Chinese people living in or even just visiting a foreign country have made before returning to their homeland.

***

Then came another essay, "The personal narrative of a literary translator," which took a long time to write and edit.[13] My first version met with severe comments from the editors, followed by suggestions as to how such the essay could be rewritten. It took a while but eventually I submitted a version that was considered acceptable.

For some years leading up to this chastisement, I'd received email requests by students in both mainland China and Hong Kong who'd presumably been advised by their teachers to contact me directly.[14] (By this time, I had my own website, which included my email address.) The requests were mostly in Chinese or poor English; some were from children who barely knew who I was or what I did. At first, I refused all such requests: some were too personal; others could be referred to my website.

In the end, I decided I was acting like a crotchety old woman and that people who took the trouble to write should be treated with respect; especially now that I'm no longer teaching, I have more time and can give them a proper response. I've also started to accept requests for interviews from Australian journalists and academics. I haven't kept a record of these requests, but one in 2015 was from someone who was obviously thoughtful and well-informed about my work, and I replied more positively. The author was Li Yi, a research student at Shanghai Jiaotong University; regarding my articles as a challenge, she arranged for us to spend a week at her university for personal interviews and discussion. Li Yi has now graduated and been appointed lecturer at the School of English Language, Literature and Culture at the Beijing International Studies University. She has also published four articles about my translations, drawing on these conversations and noting, for instance, the combination of research and translation that characterize many of my publications. Although I now rarely visit mainland China, we remain good friends.

***

Now settled in Sydney, I still miss living in Hong Kong, but there are compensations, such as relearning to speak and write Australian English. I've never gone as far as Julie Rose, the famous translator of French classics who happily adopted an unmistakably Australian voice in her translations, but my written English may have become more relaxed. Because I started out translating poetry (and for that matter, poetry written in a formal voice) I wasn't at first aware that my translation voice was inevitably formal as well, with little change between He Qifang's poems in the 1960s and Bei Dao's poems in the 1980s. I'd quickly discovered that it was not so well suited to film dialogue.

The co-translation of *Atlas* could also be regarded as having a somewhat formal written style, which fortunately corresponded to the pseudo-academic style of most of the original text. Soon after Anders joined me in Sydney in 2012, the two of us became involved in the translation of *Cantonese Love Stories* and *Catalog*. For these works, the more relaxed contemporary idiom that I by now had adopted was better suited. What neither of us expected, however, a few years on, was a totally new experience in our translation history.

In 2019, after a nomination process lasting around two years, I became one of the winners of the Special Book Award of China for that year.[15] I'd been approached by the consulate-general in Sydney to agree to my name being put forward for this award, which included a lavish cash prize plus an invitation to the award ceremony in August that year in Beijing. I was a little hesitant but argued to myself that I was not a politician (and hadn't been since I was a teenager) and my subject was simply Chinese literature. It seemed to make no difference that the main item mentioned in the formal description of my achievements was that I'd translated the Mao Zedong of 1943. It was all the same; the official Mao Zedong of 1953 was also, after all, long, long ago. No mention of Bei Dao appeared in my citation, but at that point the rights and wrongs of my record seemed irrelevant. My husband and I were able to meet some of our old friends in Beijing, we made new friends among some of the other winners, and I retain the trophy and official documentation in my university office.

Strictly speaking, Anders should have been up there with me on the podium. Fitfully during the second half of the 1970s, and thereafter increasingly more often and to greater effect, he has been the coauthor, coeditor, and/or co-translator of all of my translation and research. A belated public acknowledgement of this appears in my most recent publications,[16] and my most recent research article, still in the process of publication, is another product of our collaboration.[17]

***

To conclude, I will list the translations I am most pleased with.

Mao Zedong's *Talks at the Yan'an Forum*
Before this book appeared, there was very little in English that recognized the difference between the revised edition in 1953 and the earlier version. Here was a man leading a small, exhausted, and mostly demoralized band of mostly nonprofessional soldiers in one of the poorest and most isolated parts of rural China; how could he possibly be thinking and writing in the same way as the leader of one of the most populated countries in the world? The difference between the two versions is inevitable and principled. It remains the book that seems to be my most read.

Bei Dao's *Notes from the City of the Sun* and *The August Sleepwalker*
These two books between them made little, if any, change to the course of modern Chinese history; the poet never enjoyed the readership or the power of Mao Zedong. Nevertheless, they have been read by countless numbers of people in China and around the world, who have drawn courage and inspiration as well as pleasure from them.

Chen Kaige's *The Yellow Earth*
Chinese and non-Chinese people watching this film on its first release could hardly believe it was a film made in China, and its emotional and figurative power remains uniquely great. Its impact was the most immediate of my works.

As well, here are the translations in which I take most pride, in making my name known as a translator around the world.

He Qifang's *Paths in Dreams*
This is my first published translation and the one that made my path in China easier, even when it was already out of print.

Lu Xun and Xu Guangping's *Letters between Two*
A contribution to Lu Xun studies that has been largely ignored by English speakers, despite the huge importance this love affair made to the life and thinking of modern China's most prominent and respected writer.

Bei Dao's *The August Sleepwalker*
The poems in this early collection have been repeatedly reprinted and are still cited.

Notes

1. Powell, *A Dance to the Music of Time*, 80.
2. The first draft was a talk given at a Hong Kong translation conference in 1987, followed by presentations at the Australian National University and the University of Queensland in 1989. The final revised version was written in May 1990, shortly before I moved from Oslo to Edinburgh.
3. From March to May 2005, I published "Translation and State Power: the Peking Foreign Languages Press in the 1980s," "Genres in translation: Bringing modern Chinese literature to English-language readers," "The pains and gains of translating and being translated," "Genres in translation: Bringing modern Chinese literature to English-language readers," and "Translating and being translated in Beijing: Personal transactions in the 1980s."
4. McDougall, "Literary Translation: The Pleasure Principle," "Reading pleasures: on translating Hong Kong poetry," and "Strategic Pleasures: the uses of illustration in translating Hong Kong poetry."
5. McDougall, "Literary Translation: The Pleasure Principle."
6. Robert Wechsler, *Performing Without a Stage*, esp. 25.
7. This article has not been published.
8. According to *Xinhua*, the state news agency, ten minutes of footage containing Chow Yun-fat's 20-minute portrayal of Sao Feng ("Howling Wind") were cut for the film's release in China. One explanation was that the censored scenes involved "too much violence and horror"; another indicated that the character offered a negative and stereotypical portrayal of the Chinese people (Associated Press, June 15, 2007). Neither of these reasons explain the omission of Li Bai's "The Moon Shining Over the Mountain on the Border." Chow is said to have relished playing the role, even giving crew members a hand with props.
9. This paper has not been published.
10. The expression "cultural cringe" refers to Australian intellectuals regarding their own cultural products as inferior to anything from England and the United States.
11. McDougall, "My Hopes for the Critics," "On Conducting Ourselves as Fathers Today," "What Happens after Nora Walks Out," 194–196, 127–139, 256–262. (A short discussion on these essays appears in chapter 6.)
12. McDougall, "Xu Zhimo."

13. This had been commissioned for the *Routledge Handbook of Chinese Translation*.
14. I've not received any such invitation from Taiwan, presumably because I've never translated any Taiwan works; I believe this omission was inadvertent rather than for political reasons.
15. I haven't managed to express my view on this clumsy title for several reasons, but I would prefer something along the lines of "the Outstanding Books of the Year on Chinese Culture and Society."
16. McDougall, "Intuition and Spontaneity in Multiple Voice Literary Translation."
17. McDougall, "The Uncertainty Principle in Literary Theory."

Chapter 16

We Own Our Own Words

This chapter offers commentary on some practical matters that have affected me or questions that have been asked of me; other translators may face them too. I dare not suggest that anyone should copy my choices, but perhaps these remarks may be of interest, especially to those just setting out.

How do you choose who or what to translate?
I've been asked this question a lot over the past fifty years, and the answers have usually differed. As I wrote the preceding chapters, I imagined a pattern emerging and am tempted to claim that I have not so much chosen what to translate as having responded to choices thrust upon me. As a beginner in my late twenties, I'd accepted being given my first major translation subject (He Qifang's poetry and essays), although I didn't adopt the approach that was recommended. The next big project (translation of the first published version of Mao Zedong's Yan'an Talks) was an unexpected discovery, and friends and colleagues encouraged me to take it on. Beginning to see myself in this role, I applied for a job as a professional translator; after three years so employed, I finally developed confidence in making independent choices.

My next major project (translation of Bei Dao's poetry and fiction) began with the oddest set of circumstances provided by a young Chinese woman, but it came to include all phases of translation activity, from choosing which person and which work to translate to selecting the publisher and promoting the work sometimes beyond standard academic experience. Some of these phases were affected by political necessity of a high order. A follow-up project was sparked by Sun Jialin, wife of the budding film director, Chen Kaige: the result was the translation of two film scripts. It was also during this period that I was translating Ah Cheng's three stories.

Through these projects, I'd achieved some public recognition as a literary translator, encouraging invitations from publishers and the recovery of a modern Chinese masterpiece neglected for some twenty years. Approaching retirement, I began my Hong Kong phase, which involved selecting local materials for teaching translation leading to the discovery of a gifted but complex writer, whose translation required drawing on the multiple expertise of my husband, Anders. My final undertaking, which involved switching languages and translating from Swedish into English, began with a request from an old friend and led to cooperation with Anders in a project where I was a stumbling beginner and he the native expert. In short, my career as a translator has been based on decisions that were naive, accidental, and only in a small number of cases selected by me at my own initiative.

I would not necessarily advise a young translator to marry someone whose language was not your own; to spend a few years in an elite institution regardless of whether you are getting paid; to spend another few years in the country of your translation language without bothering to consider its competing claims on your own beliefs; to hold fast to your conviction that you know what your readers to be want and need to know...and so on. Yet I stumbled into most of these states without being particularly aware of what I was doing. Maybe most of these choices were in the end justified, but I suppose my best decision was to live to the age of eighty two so that I have plenty to reminisce about as I drift into a translation-free zone—at least translation from Chinese to English.

Can you make a living from literary translation?
No.

To what extent has politics affected your choice of works to translate?
One lasting effect of my first stay in China was that without declaring this either to myself or to others, I'd chosen literature over politics. It's true that in the last and present centuries Chinese literature has been saturated with politics, and politics have certainly influenced my choice of translatees and their works, but I've stayed away from active political choices: I don't choose or accept for translation a work solely on the basis of its political messages.

What kind of relationships have you had with your translatees?
Some I never met. Some became close friends. Most relationships were conducted with goodwill on both sides but not intimacy. As I've repeatedly noted, chance, luck, opportunity, and contingency form the basis of my largely haphazard strategies for finding potential translatees.

What theory or theories affect your translations?
I became aware of the usefulness of translation theories in the 1990s. Since then, they've certainly made translation studies more sophisticated. I try to set aside all thoughts about theories when I'm actually translating, however. In the 2000s, I proposed the slogan "the pleasure principle" as a lighthearted way to suggest that translation goals could have some kind of theoretical respectability.

How do you get an agent for your translations?

My earliest translation was part of an academic exercise, and for a long time it stayed that way; the thought of acquiring an agent just didn't cross my mind. There weren't very many of us doing Chinese literary translation at that time. The first I ever heard of the possibility of hiring an agent occurred around the turn of the century, and it seemed quite funny to me. In any case, by that time I'd become addicted to my own working style, and trying to find an agent hardly seemed worth the effort. I've had a salary (and now, a pension) just about all my life, and I haven't needed royalties or fees for my bread and butter. However, it is now more common that Chinese authors routinely acquire agents for themselves and their translators, and not bothering to do the same could be seen as willful ignorance of its benefits.

Perhaps, after all, a skillful literary agent may enable a literary translator to make a living, but this would be more likely for translations from rather than into English.

How and when do you choose a collaborator?

It's difficult to generalize on working with a collaborator: translation can be an emotional and intellectual experience in which working with another person can be invigorating, fraught, or a bit of both. It's essential that your collaborator understands your language, although such an understanding does present its own problems. What seems to work well is a collaborator who knows the translatee in person or comes from a similar background. What really doesn't work is where one translator has limited knowledge of Chinese and the other has limited knowledge of English: errors from this kind of partnership are easy to make, leading the eventual reader to stumble on passages that feel vaguely wrong but without quite knowing what would have been intended. Sometimes I've preferred to work on my own with advice from the author or other colleagues, but a formal arrangement with a co-translator can save a lot of time if that's important. My best experiences with co-translation have been with Chen Maiping and Anders Hansson.

How long does it take to translate a full-length book?
It's hard for a translator to make a reliable estimate about how long a book-length translation would take, from selecting the author or work to the finished publication, no matter what the publisher's plan is. Just selecting a work to translate may take long enough. Then, how long does it take to finish even the first draft? How long to get it ready for submission? And how long for the publisher to put it to market? Usually months, if not years, more than estimated. Sometimes all stages go smoothly, but I've experienced only a handful of instances when that happened. Holding down a full-time job while taking on a book-length translation may result in poor outcomes for both, but an academic post where translation can be part of your recognized workload seems to work. Otherwise, I don't know if there's any reliable solution for either translator or publisher.

Have you used radio or television to promote your translations?
I haven't really cut it as a radio or TV performer. In 1992 I took part in a program called *Bookshelf* on BBC Radio 4 with a short talk on the subject "Poetry in Chinese"; I haven't a copy of it myself but it's in the British Library Sound holdings. I've also taken part in radio or television broadcasts in Beijing and in Hong Kong, but none seem to have made any sort of impact. With some exceptions, as in the case of Bei Dao's early poetry, I've left it up to the publisher to engage with the media.

Which do you prefer: research or translation?
That's like asking whether I prefer the company of men or women. I don't think there's any sensible answer.

How do you set about drafting your translations?
If your translatee is dead, you're on your own. If your translatee is alive but unapproachable, you do your best, hoping it won't cause problems. If your translatee is approachable, it's a gift to be treasured, but it can also

be troublesome. There's a huge advantage in being able to pose questions on meaning and style. If your translatee knows the translation language, however, even the most agreeable of them may fail to understand that it is the translation that is being published and that their intrusion may be unwanted. Then other problems arise.

What kind of problems have generally affected your practice in translation?

Some matters requiring solutions, which seem to me quite reasonable, may not be possible in practice. For example,

Who should choose a book title: the translatee, the publisher, or the translator?

First, not the translatee, who should stick to their own books and have little or no say in their translation. The publisher has the better claim, having at least some idea of what may appeal to the potential readership. The easiest solution for the translator is simply to translate the title closely, hoping the publisher will accept it, but what works in one language doesn't necessarily work in another. One solution could be to adopt a free translation for the cover and title page, with a close translation added in brackets alongside the original title on the verso page (I haven't actually done this, but it seems a useful ploy). In short, this is the kind of problem that translators have to deal with every time they're involved in making a translation, but it's significant every time, given that they're dealing with the title.

Who should design the cover?

Professional publishers have their own resources, but it's essential that the translator be consulted (the case of Ah Cheng's *Three Kings* and *King of Trees* is an egregious example of wholly inappropriate design). Again, the translatee may be consulted but, unlike the publisher, should not have the final word. (With the exception of the cover for *Paths in Dreams*, I've never been the sole voice in determining the physical production

We Own Our Own Words

or appearance of any of my books. There may have been cases where I was shown the book cover, but it was not for me to choose or modify it: the translatee and the publisher are stronger voices. Large publishers, of course, usually have professional designers, but the design should always serve the reading experience.)

What should always appear on the cover?
Publishers may flinch but the translator's name should always be featured, large or small. (One of my covers, discussed previously, failed even to indicate that a translation of a film was the major content in the book or to mention the translator's name. Perhaps, in that particular instance, I should be regarded as lucky.)

What should always appear on the title page?
Again, the translator's name should always appear on the title page. Where there are two or more translators, the name of the translator who produced the final version should come first and most prominently unless there are strong reasons otherwise. (A designer's suggestion that "it looks better" to omit the name or change the name order is not a strong reason.)

These comments may sound picky, but whatever the length of the translation, the text is in the words of the translator: how else, otherwise, are our translations given our due? How else are translations to be valued? And how else is the translator's name to become recognized? Above all, when will it be admitted that we own our own words?

What is the most difficult item or aspect in any translation?
Beyond doubt, a book's title, more than any other part of the text, is the most difficult text to translate. This may be well known, but I've still fallen into traps. Sometimes the translator isn't even invited to supply the title, the translatee or the publisher having stepped in without any consultation. The trickiest case that I've been involved in is the translation of Ah Cheng's fiction, all parties, including me, being responsible for

poor decisions. Let's start with my suggestion: *Three Kings*. I have noted in chapter 10 how my ignorance of biblical terminology resulted in this title being confusing. Here, as also in chapter 8, I would like to point out in this sorry tale how easy it is for an inexperienced translator to be trapped by the infinite variety of meanings in both Chinese and English.

Again, most translators know that one of the trickiest problems in translating from Chinese to English is that Chinese for the most part omits the use of definite articles before nouns. There are some indications for when definite articles should be omitted in translation: for instance, the position of a noun before the verb is more likely to indicate the definite case than a noun in the predicate, but this is not a rule. I used to find it easy, but the more I read and the more I translate, I can't claim infallibility in the use of "the." I've just been reading the last two volumes of Anthony Powell's *A Dance to the Music of Time* and noticed a lot of examples where I would have used the definite article but where it didn't appear. Powell is a master writer, and I must defer to his example. (The two volumes were published in 1973 and 1975 but can't really be considered out of date.)

Which is more effective in leading to the understanding of a foreign literature, translation or academic research?

When it comes to increasing our understanding of Chinese literature, this is a foolish question, for who can measure the result of either? My experience is that translation is a valuable aid to understanding a literary text, and I'm tempted to claim that it is necessary, but there is no way to compare and test this simple assertion. What I do believe is that translation aids our comprehension of language and literary texts, whichever language is being read in whichever literary work.

We Own Our Own Words

Does translating set off research, or does research lead to translation?
It can happen either way. Translating Bei Dao led to research on his work and the cultural history of the time; research on He Qifang's poetry and essays led to translating them, and eventually translating took over.

Which promotes a better understanding of a text: translating it or comparing the difference between earlier and later versions?
It depends on the circumstances. In the case of Mao's *"Talks,"* both come into play. In the case of He Qifang, the later versions point to political pressure but are not enlightening in understanding his poetry.

Is there such a thing as an ideal physical location for translators?
I am forever in debt to A. R. Davis and to the University of Sydney's Fisher Library for stocking materials from the new literary movements in China; only a huge resource such as the Harvard-Yenching Library would offer forgotten pamphlets of great importance; only in Hong Kong would I be able to understand the difficulties of Hong Kong writers. That said, the advent in 2015 of the Paper Republic and its more recent Paper Republic Translation Database has been of inestimable value to new and older Chinese-English literary translators and translation readers, and all of us are indebted to the founder, Eric Abrahamsen, and his colleagues. Physical location is still a factor in translation, but its impact is becoming less important.

What kind of sources can the translator turn to?
I should never forget that my good fortune in obtaining translation-worthy materials was to a large extent due to, first, the misfortunes of those Chinese readers who sold their precious home collections of twentieth-century writing directly or indirectly in Hong Kong during the 1960s and 1970s and, then, those young writers in the late 1970s and

early 1980s who dared to pass on or sometimes sell their work to eager buyers from abroad.

    Until very recently, Hong Kong had been the most fruitful place to obtain firsthand some of the most outstanding work of Chinese writers of twentieth- and twenty-first-century literature. At present, its future is uncertain.

Does living in a series of different countries or cities help being a translator?

In my case, I went from Sydney to Beijing, back to Sydney, then to Cambridge, from there to Beijing again, on to Oslo, then to Edinburgh, then to Hong Kong, and finally back to Sydney, where I expect to stay for the rest of my years. Maybe the change of place did matter; as new friends and colleagues meet and form friendships, new ideas and opportunities emerge, but old friends and colleagues also provide a raft of consolation and hope. In any case, improving my translation techniques hasn't been a reason for finding new places to work and rest. Both push and pull sent me to difference places, but all were large cities with extensive university libraries. Libraries have always been a treasured accompaniment to research and an even more relaxing source of pleasure. I hope they never disappear.

Is any one place better to live in than another for literary translation?

Dabbling in literary translation was initially for me more a matter of timing than locality, but living abroad and changing places may have been an advantage. This is pretty obvious, but every place has its benefits and shortcomings: Harvard was not an encouraging place to translate Chinese poetry; Sydney would probably have been better then. Beijing was an excellent place for translation because in the early to mid-1980s it was relatively easy to get to know writers and their works (e.g., hanging out in student cafes and other academic playgrounds). Edinburgh was not particularly encouraging, but Hong Kong, like Beijing, was immensely stimulating. For me, returning to Sydney was also productive. That said, university-based translation studies courses don't necessarily correlate to productivity in literary translation. The benefits of well-stocked libraries are probably indispensable, but translation-studies courses (whether teaching them or being taught) aren't; actual literary translation is not dependent on the latter any more than a university education makes a superior literary writer. Nor is it necessarily the case that knowing writers personally makes a good translation a better one or that contemporary writing always makes better translation.

Translators are best bilingual, but what about being multilingual?

Apart from the languages I learned at school, I attended a one-year course in Old Norse at Harvard and became a beginner in modern Swedish at home. In Norway I was obliged to study Norwegian for my first year of employment there and for about three years spoke four languages more or less daily; in Edinburgh I toyed with the idea of learning Scottish Gaelic but drew back just in time; and in Hong Kong I took lessons in Cantonese but failed to become proficient. At no point did I give any thought to translating from any of these languages except Mandarin Chinese into English or to translating from English into Chinese, except very briefly and recently when I've co-translated from Swedish to English. I've now lost a lot of my translation proficiency, but it's been for other reasons.

I think it's a bonus in every way to know lots of languages, preferably not all of them in one language family, but I remain convinced that as a rule it is best to translate into one's native language and to cultivate that language as best one can.

What are the factors that most influenced your choice of works or authors to translate?

Looking back at works by the fifty-odd writers I've translated, I'm struck by the variety of these transactions and their haphazard occurrence. My choice has sometimes been made before I ever knew the author or had read any of their works. In retrospect, most of the choices regarding the genre, the intended audience, and the financial gain from publication seem either determined by others or else purely accidental or coincidental. However, if I had to nominate factors that have been more or less constant, the first would be the advice I've received from others.

What do you consider to be your main contribution to disseminating knowledge of China?

I've wanted to emphasize the importance of knowing and cultivating one's own cultural heritage at the same time as teaching and researching Chinese history and culture. I've also wanted to convey that China does not consist of one language, one culture, and one people, but many different strands of each of these and for the most part managing to coexist. (My translations don't really contribute to this.) As teachers we tend to stress the differences between the Chinese languages, cultures, and people and our own (Australian, English-speaking or roughly Western), whereas in research we're more likely to stress what we have in common or overlapping interests. I'm not sure how literary translation affects any of these things but hope in some way that it does.

How has translation changed your life?

It was when I was translating poetry first by He Qifang and twenty years later by Bei Dao that I became aware that these writers were influencing my own thoughts and emotions. This subtle but profound influence seems in hindsight almost inevitable in poetry translation. Even when I switched to prose, to some extent I still quite unconsciously began to absorb the writers' literary persona. I was on the side of the still-youthful rebel Mao Zedong at his remote military base, speaking with little concern for the sensitivities of the intellectuals and writers who sought his leadership, but somehow I was also able to admire his dramatic transformation into the leader of one of the world's biggest countries. Later, translating their letters, I began to side with Xu Guangping while appreciating the reasons for Lu Xun's diffidence in their long affair. Even in the most difficult stretches in my financially strapped undergraduate years, I never suffered the deprivations experienced by Ah Cheng, but I still believed I could understand the pressures he was under, detached while ill at ease in an almost incomprehensible society. In different ways and to different effect, these writers' words on a page became blended with my own beliefs.

Any hints for tactical translations?
Some tactical hints for literary translation (with apologies for the mixed metaphors):

- work on the bones; let the flesh take care of itself
- open the toy box as well as the toolbox
- ignore ready-made solutions; handcraft your own
- trust the consumer, not the producer

The main thing is to look after your health and walk a lot.

When is it time to give up translating?
Maybe when you start writing books about yourself.

CONCLUSION

It's only as I've been writing this narrative that I've become aware of the relationships, personal and literary, that led me to translate and to arrange for the translations to be published. For as long as I can remember, I've been an avid reader. Our local municipal council had a library conveniently located between both of my two primary schools and home. The librarians were very kind, so I was allowed to carry out some basic library duties such as shelving books. When I ran out of books in the children's section, I was allowed access to the young adult collection, although there were still several years to go before I was technically allowed there. And then my mother worked in a left-wing bookshop, where I was welcome to read whatever I found of interest.

When my family moved to a city south of Sydney I was not so well provided for, although there was also free access to all sorts of scattered collections where I worked during the holidays. At Peking University, I soon became a dedicated borrower, writing down the title and author of all the books I was able to find there. After returning from China in 1959, I found a full-time position in Wollongong City Library, where I learned the basics of being a librarian and borrowed as much from their collection as I could carry home. When I moved back to Sydney, I had the University of Sydney libraries at my disposal, and the peak of my library use was achieved when I worked for the better part of a year at the Oriental collection at the university's Fisher Library.

It has always seemed to me that an obsession with books was a necessary condition for competence with translations in general and literary works in particular. Now that printed books are rapidly being taken over by online texts, I assume that translators will take to the latter beautifully, but I expect that printed books and the libraries that store them will continue to be a translator's joy and treasure.

***

Looking at some of my translations today, I wish it were possible to rewrite some of them: sentences, phrases, and words seem stilted, and I'd prefer to replace them with something more informal. After I moved to China, I stopped speaking and reading English all day every day. At home, I spoke in Swedish to our young son, although I still spoke English to my husband and our Swedish friends. To our Chinese friends and others I encountered every day (including, for example, the staff in shops and restaurants), I spoke Chinese. I still had access to books in English, but I was reading and translating Chinese every day. In Edinburgh I probably recovered some facility with English but may have lost some of it again when we moved to Hong Kong.

We Own Our Own Words

Now I'm back in an Australian English environment, read English much more often than Chinese, and have few friends who can only converse in Chinese. Do I intend to rewrite my earlier translations? No.

If you have gotten as far as this, dear reader, you would have noticed how many times the word "grateful" has appeared previously, and it is undeniable that I owe a lot to the people who have helped with translations and their publication since 1976. You may also have been irritated by my persistence in recording when my name appeared on the front cover and on the title page, and how indignant I became when they were relegated to a secondary position. I make no apology for this. The legal status of these books and shorter contributions may lie with the publisher, but I am the author of the translation, and both praise and blame for it rest with me.

Appendix

Photo 1: An outing with FLP colleagues to the Fragrant Hills, west of Beijing, in October 1980, soon after my arrival in China.

Appendix

Photo 2: The FLP English Section on the way to the Temple of Azure Clouds, Beijing, April 1981.

Photo 3: The FLP English Section on an outing to the botanical gardens of Beijing in 1981.

Photo 4: My colleague Zhu Peiyu with my son, Torkel, and me at the Foreign Languages Press (FLP) office in Beijing in October 1982.

Photo 5: My son, Torkel, and me on an FLP spring outing at the lake in the Purple Bamboo Park in Beijing in May 1983.

Appendix

Photo 6: The FLP English Section on an outing to the Purple Bamboo Park in October 1983.

Photo 7: My son, Torkel, and me on a visit to the office where my husband, Anders, worked in Beijing in 1984/1985.

Appendix

Photo 8: With Bei Dao in Beijing. Photo taken between 1982 and 1985.

Photo 9: With Bei Dao in Hong Kong in 2009.

Appendix 241

Photo 10: With Bei Dao in Hong Kong in 2009.

Photo 11: With Chinese University of Hong Kong (CUHK) class in Hong Kong in 2006.

Appendix

Photo 12: CUHK excursion in Hong Kong in 2006.

Photo 13: With colleagues from City University of Hong Kong in Hong Kong in 2009.

Appendix

Photo 14: The 13th Special Book Awards of China ceremony in Beijing in 2019.

Chronology of Publications by Bonnie S. McDougall

Books

The Introduction of Western Literary Theories into China, 1919-1925. Tokyo: Centre for East Asian Cultural Studies, 1971.

Paths in Dreams: Selected Prose and Poetry of Ho Ch'i-fang. Translated and edited with an introduction and afterword by Bonnie S. McDougall. Brisbane: University of Queensland Press, 1976.

* "Afterword" in *Paths in Dreams: Selected Prose and Poetry of Ho Ch'i-fang.* Translated into Chinese by Zhou Faxiang. *Wenxue yanjiu dongtai* [Journal of the Literature Institute of the Chinese Academy of Social Sciences] 2 (January 1980): 21–33. of Social Sciences] 2 (January 1980): 21–33.

Mao Zedong's Talks at the Yan'an Conference on Literature and Art. Translated and edited with an introduction by Bonnie S. McDougall. Ann Arbor: Center for Chinese Studies, University of Michigan, 1980.

Notes from the City of the Sun: Poems by Bei Dao. Translated and edited with an introduction by Bonnie S. McDougall. Ithaca : Cornell University China-Japan Program, 1983.

Literature and the Arts. Co-translated with Liuyu Hu. China Handbook series. Beijing: Foreign Languages Press, 1983.

Popular Chinese Literature and Performing Arts in the People's Republic of China, 1949-1979. Edited with an introduction by Bonnie S. McDougall. Berkeley: University of California Press, 1984. Reprinted as paperback in the Voices series 2018.

Lu Xun, A Biography by Wang Shiqing. Translated by Zhang Peiji. English text co-edited with Tang Bowen. Beijing: Foreign Languages Press, 1984.

The Yongle Palace Murals. Co-translated with Zhang Xinglian. Beijing: Foreign Languages Press, 1985.

Chestnuts and Other Stories by Xiao Qian. Edited by Bonnie S. McDougall and co-translated with Xiao Qian, Elisabeth Eide, and Xiong Zhenru. Beijing: Panda Books, 1985.

Bodong (Waves) by Zhao Zhenkai. Edited with an introduction by Bonnie S. McDougall. Hong Kong: The Chinese University Press, 1985.

Waves by Zhao Zhenkai. Edited and co-translated with Susette Ternent Cooke with an introduction by Bonnie S. McDougall. Hong Kong: The Chinese University Press, 1985. Revised and expanded ed., 1986.

King of the Children by Chen Kaige. Edited and translated by Bonnie S. McDougall. London: Faber and Faber, 1989.

Waves by Bei Dao. Edited and co-translated with Susette Ternent Cooke an introduction by Bonnie S. McDougall. London: Heinemann, 1987. Paperback ed., Sceptre: London, 1989. Revised North American ed., New York: New Directions, 1990.

The August Sleepwalker by Bei Dao. Edited and translated with an introduction by Bonnie S. McDougall. London: Anvil Press, 1988. (This is the revised and expanded edition of *Notes from the City of the Sun* cited earlier). Revised North American ed., New Directions, New York, 1990.

The King of Trees by Ah Cheng. Translated with an Afterword by Bonnie S. McDougall. New York: New Directions, 1990 [2010].

Three Kings: Three Stories from Today's China by Ah Cheng. Edited and translated with an introduction by Bonnie S. McDougall. London: Collins Harvill, 1990.

The Yellow Earth: A Film by Chen Kaige. Hong Kong: The Chinese University Press, 1991.

Old Snow by Bei Dao. Co-translated with Chen Maiping, with preface by Bonnie S. McDougall. New York: New Directions, 1991. British ed. published by London: Anvil Press Poetry, 1992.

Brocade Valley by Wang Anyi. Co-translated with Chen Maiping, with an introduction by Bonnie S. McDougall. New York: New Directions, 1992.

The Literature of China in the Twentieth Century. Coauthored with Kam Louie. New York: Hurst & Columbia University Press, 1997.

Lu Xun and Xu Guangping, Letters between Two. Translated and edited by Bonnie S. McDougall, Beijing: Foreign Languages Press, 2000. Index published in *Modern Chinese Literature and Culture Resource Center* (February 2004). http://mclc.osu.edu/rc/pubs/index.htm.

Chinese Concepts of Privacy. Coedited with Anders Hansson. Leiden: Brill, 2002.

The Chinese at Play: Festivals, Games and Leisure. Coedited with Anders Hansson and Frances Weightman. London: Kegan Paul, 2002.

Love-letters and Privacy in Modern China: The Intimate Lives of Lu Xun and Xu Guangping. Oxford: Oxford University Press, 2002.

Fictional Authors, Imaginary Audiences: Modern Chinese Literature in the Twentieth Century. Hong Kong: Chinese University Press, 2003. * "Crossdressing in modern Chinese fiction, drama and film: Chen Kaige's 'Farewell My Concubine'" in *Fictional Authors, Imaginary Audiences: Modern Chinese Literature in the Twentieth Century*. Translated into Chinese in *Ba wang bie ji: tongzhi yuedu yu kuawenhua duihua* [Farewell My Concubine: Same-sex readings and crosscultural dialogues], edited by Chen Ya-chen. Chia-yi: Nan Hua University Press, 2004.

The King of Trees by Ah Cheng. Edited and translated with an afterword by Bonnie S. McDougall. Rev. ed. of *Three Kings*. New York: New Directions, 2010.

Translation Zones in Modern China: Authoritarian Command Versus Gift Exchange. Amherst, NY: Cambria Press, 2011.

Atlas: The Archeology of an Imaginary City by Dung Kai-cheung [Dong Qizhang]. Co-translated with Dung Kai-cheung and Anders Hansson, with an introduction by Bonnie S. McDougall. New York: Columbia University Press, 2012.

Cantonese Love Stories: Twenty-five Vignettes of a City by Dung Kai-cheung. Co-translated with Anders Hansson. Sydney: Penguin Special, 2017.

A Catalog of Such Stuff as Dreams Are Made On by Dung Kai-cheung. Co-translated with Anders Hansson. New York: Columbia University Press, 2022.

Translation Stories from Modern China. Amherst, NY: Cambria Press, 2024.

Chapters in Books (All Invited Contributions)

"The Search for Synthesis: T'ien Han and Mao Tun in the 1920s." In *Search for Identity: Literature and the Creative Arts in Asia*, edited by A. R. Davis, 225–254. Sydney: Angus & Robertson, 1974.

"The View from the Leaning Tower: Zhu Guangqian on Aesthetics and Society in the Nineteen-twenties and Thirties." In *Modern Chinese Literature and its Social Context*, edited by Göran Malmqvist, 76–122. Stockholm: Nobel Symposium No. 32, 1977. * Chinese translation in *Xin wenxue shiliao* 3 (1981).

"Västerlandets litterära inflytande." In *Hundens År: Årsbok om Kina*, Harriet Johansson et al. eds., 76–86. Södertälje: Svensk-kinesiska vänskapsförbundet, 1982.

"The Impact of Western Literary Trends." In *Modern Chinese Literature in the May Fourth Era*, edited by Merle Goldman, 37–61. Cambridge, MA: Harvard University Press, 1977. * Chinese translation in *Zhongguo xiandai wenxue yanjiu congkan* 1 (1983).

"Writers and Performers, Their Works, and Their Audiences in the First Three Decades." In *Popular Chinese Literature and Performing Arts in the People's Republic of China, 1949-1979*, edited by Bonnie S. McDougall, 269–304. Berkeley: University of California Press, 1984.

"Quest and Confrontation: The Poetic and Fictional Voices of Bei Dao/Zhao Zhenkai." In *Vägar till Kina: Göran Malmqvist 60 år.*, edited by Bert Edström et al., 14–18. Orientaliska studier 49–50. Stockholm: Torbjörn Lodén, 1984.

"The Third Phase: Reflections on the Smolenice Symposium on May Fourth Literature." In *Interliterary and Intraliterary Aspects of the May Fourth Movement 1919 in China: Proceedings of the international sinological symposium, Smolenice Castle, March 13-17, 1989*, edited by M. Galik, 265–268. Bratislava: VEDA, Publishing House of the Slovak Academy of Science, 1990.

"Censorship & Self-Censorship in Contemporary Chinese Literature." In *After the Event: Human Rights and their Future in China*, edited by Susan Whitfield, 73–90. London: Wellsweep Press, 1993.

"The Anxiety of Out-fluence: Creativity, History and Postmodernity." In *Inside Out: Modernism and Postmodernism in Chinese Literary Culture*, edited by Wendy Larson and Anne Wedell-Wedellsborg, 99–112. Aarhus: Aarhus University Press, 1993.

"Modern Chinese Literature and Its Critics." In *European Association of Chinese Studies: Selected Papers of the 10th Biannual Conference*, edited by Lucie Borotova. Prague: Charles University, 1996.

"Dominance and Disappearance: A Post-Feminist Review of Fiction by Mao Dun and Ling Shuhua." In *Autumn Floods: Essays in Honour of Marian Galik*, edited by Raoul D. Findeisen and Robert H. Gassman, 283–306. Bern: Peter Lang, 1998.

"Literary Decorum or Carnivalistic Grotesque: Literature in the PRC after 50 Years." In *The People's Republic of China After 50 Years*, edited by Richard Louis Edmonds, 161–170. Oxford: Oxford University Press, 2000.

"Lu Xun Hates China, Lu Xun Hates Lu Xun." In *Symbols of Anguish: In Search of Melancholy in China*, edited by Wolfgang Kubin, 385–400. Bern: Peter Lang, 2001.

"Brotherly love: Lu Xun, Zhou Zuoren and Zhou Jianren." In *China in seinen biographischen Dimensionen: Gedenkschrift für Helmut Martin*, edited by Christina Neder et al., 259–276. Wiesbaden: Harrassowitz Verlag, 2001.

"Particulars and Universals: Studies on Chinese Privacy." In *Chinese Concepts of Privacy*, edited by Bonnie S. McDougall and Anders Hansson, 2–24.

"Functions and Values of Privacy in the Correspondence between Lu Xun and Xu Guangping, 1925-1929." In *Chinese Concepts of Privacy*, edited by Bonnie S. McDougall and Anders Hansson, 147–168.

"Revealing to Conceal: Love-letters and Privacy in Republican China." In *Concealing to Reveal: An International Scholarly Conference on "the Private" and "Sentiment" in Chinese History and Culture*. Vol. 2 , *Sentiment*, edited by Ping-chen Hsiung, 279–346. Taipei: Center for Chinese Studies, 2003. * Abstract published in Newsletter *for Research in Chinese Studies* 20, no. 2 (May 2001): 103–104.

"Privacy." In *New Dictionary of the History of Ideas*. Vol. 5, edited by Maryanne Cline Horowitz, 1899–1907. Detroit: Charles Scribner's Sons, 2005.

"Diversity as Value: Marginality, Post-colonialism and Identity in Modern Chinese Literature." In *Belief, History and the Individual in Modern Chinese Literary Culture*, edited by Artur K. Wardega, 137–165. Cambridge: Cambridge Scholars Publishing, 2009.

"Shen Congwen en la literatura contemporánea China" [Shen Congwen and contemporary Chinese literature]. Translated into Spanish by Yolanda Fontal, in *La ciudad fronteriza* [The border town], 13–50. Barcelona: Edicions Bellaterra, 2013.

"Infinite Variations of Writing and Desire: Love Letters in China and Europe." In *A History of Chinese Letters and Epistolary Culture*, edited by Antje Richter, 546–581. Leiden: Brill, 2015.

"Lu Xun Travels around the World: From Beijing, Oslo and Sydney to Cambridge Mass." In *Lu Xun and Australia*, edited by Mabel Lee, Chiu-yee Cheung, and Sue Wiles, 126–130. Sydney: Australian Scholarship, 2016.

"Hong Kong's Literary Retrocession in Three Fantastical Novels." In *A New Literary History of Modern China*, edited by David Der-wei Wang, 856–861. Cambridge: Harvard University Press, 2017. * Features studies on Lilian Lee's *Yanzhi kou*, Wong Bik Wan's *Doomsday Hotel*, and Dung Kai-cheung's *Atlas* (1997).

"The personal narrative of a Chinese literary translator." In *The Routledge Handbook of Chinese Translation*, edited by Chris Shei and Zhao-Ming Gao, 388–400. London: Routledge, 2018.

"Xu Zhimo." In *Into English: Poems, Translations, Commentaries*, edited Martha Collins and Kevin Prufer, 113–120. Minneapolis: Graywolf Press, 2017.

"Intuition and spontaneity in multiple voice literary translation: Collaboration by accident or design." In *A Century of Chinese Literature in Translation (1919–2019): English Publication and Reception*, edited by Leah Gerber and Lintao Qi, 41–56. London: Routledge, 2020.

"Perceptions of Power in Literary Translation: Translators and translatees." In *The Bloomsbury Handbook of Modern Chinese Literature in Translation*, edited by Cosima Bruno, Lucas Klein, and Chris Song, 155–166. London: Bloomsbury Academic, 2024.

"The Uncertainty Principle in Literary Theory: Personal and Political Self-censorship." In *A Hundred Years of Enlightenment in China: Revisiting the May Fourth New Culture Movement*, edited by Torbjörn Lodén. Stockholm: Kungl. Vitterhets historie och antikvitets akademien, forthcoming.

Journal Articles (Refereed)

"European Influences in the Poetry of Ho Ch'i-fang." *Journal of the Oriental Society of Australia* 5, nos. 1 & 2 (December 1967).

"The Importance of Being Earnest in China: Early Chinese Attitudes towards Oscar Wilde." *JOSA* 9, nos. 1 & 2 (1972–1973): 84–98.

"Poems, Poets, and Poetry 1976: An Exercise in the Typology of Modern Chinese Literature." *Contemporary China* 2, no. 4 (Winter 1978): 76–124.

"Dissent Literature: Official and Nonofficial Literature In and About China in the Seventies." *Contemporary China* 3, no. 4 (Winter 1979): 49–79.

"Underground Literature: Two Reports from Hong Kong." *Contemporary China.* 3, no. 4 (Winter 1979): 80–90.

"Memories and Metamorphoses of a Thirties' Intellectual: A Study of He Qifang's 'Old Men' (Lao ren)." *Chinese Literature: Essays, Articles, Reviews* 3, no. 1 (January 1981).

"Zhao Zhenkai's Fiction: A Study in Cultural Alienation." *Modern Chinese Literature* 1, no. 1 (September 1984): 103–130.

"Bei Dao's Poetry: Revelation and Communication." *Modern Chinese Literature* 1, no. 2 (Spring 1985): 225–257.

"Breaking Through: Literature and the Arts in China 1976-1986." *Copenhagen Papers in East and Southeast Asian Studies* 1 (1988) (not refereed): 35–65.

"Problems and Possibilities in Translating Contemporary Chinese Literature." *Australian Journal of Chinese Affairs*, no. 25 (January 1991): 37–67.

"Wailai yingxiang de jiaolü: chuangzaoxing, lishi yu hou-xiandaixing" [The Anxiety of Out-fluence: Creativity, History and Post-Modernism], *Jintian* [Today], no. 3/4 (1991): 86–93. (not refereed).

"Cross-Dressing and the Disappearing Woman in Modern Chinese Fiction, Drama and Film: Reflections on Chen Kaige's *Farewell My Concubine.*" *China Information* 8, no. 4 (Spring 1994): 42–51 (invited and therefore not refereed).

"Modern Chinese Poetry." *Modern Chinese Literature* 8, nos. 1 & 2 (Spring/Fall 1994): 127–170.

"Self-Narrative as Group Discourse: Female Subjectivity in Wang Anyi's Fiction." *Asian Studies Review* 19, no. 2 (November 1995): 1–24.

"Chinese Errors and English Infelicities." *Journal of Macrolinguistics* 6 & 7 (January 1996): 11–21.

"Writing Self: Author/Audience Complicity in Modern Chinese Fiction." *Archiv Orientalni* 64, no. 2 (1996): 245–268.

"Disappearing Women and Disappearing Men in May Fourth Narrative: a Post-feminist Survey of Short Stories by Mao Dun, Bing Xin, Ling

Shuhua and Shen Congwen." *Asian Studies Review* 22, no. 4 (December 1998): 427–458.

"Literary Decorum or Carnivalistic Grotesque: Literature in the PRC after 50 years." *China Quarterly*, no. 159 (September 1999): 723–732.

"Privacy in Contemporary China: A Survey of Student Opinion, June 2000." *China Information* 15, no. 2 (2001): 140–152.

"Privacy in Modern China." *History Compass* 2 (2005), no. 1. https://compass.onlinelibrary.wiley.com/doi/10.1111/j.1478-0542.2004.00097.x

"Discourse on Privacy by Chinese Women Writers in Late Twentieth Century China." *China Information* 19, no. 1 (March 2005): 97–119.

"Yingyu shijie yinsi gainian zongshu" 英语世界隐私概念總述 [Concepts of privacy in the English-speaking world, summary]. In *Nankai xuebao: zhexue shehui kexue ban* 南开学报 (哲学社会科学版) (Jan. 2005): 32–42.

"Privacy Concepts, Values and Terminology in Hong Kong Fiction." In *Institute of Chinese Studies Visiting Professor Lecture Series 1*, 107–167. Hong Kong: The Chinese University of Hong Kong, 2005.

"Enduring Fascination, Untutored Understanding: Love Letters in China and Europe." *Monumenta Serica* 54 (2006): 195–206.

"Literary Translation: The Pleasure Principle." *Chinese Translators Journal* 28, no. 185 (October 2007): 22–26.

"Zuowei jiazhi de duoyangxing: bianyuanxing, houzhiminzhuyi yu Zhongguo xiandai wenxue zhong de shenfen tezheng" [Diversity as value: marginality, post-colonialism and identity in modern Chinese literature]. Translated by Fan Hua. *Shijie Hanyu* [World literature] 10 (2012): 193–206.

"Ambiguities of power: the social space of translation relationships." *Journal of the Oriental Society of Australia* 44 (2012): 1–15.

"Zhongguo dangdai wenxue, quanqiu wenhua yu fanyi" [Contemporary Chinese literature, global culture and translation]. *Shijie Hanyu* [World sinology] 13 (2014): 143–151.

"World literature, global culture and contemporary Chinese literature in translation." *International Communication of Chinese Culture* (June 2014).

"Qiaohe haishi guyi: fuheshi wenxue fanyi zhong de zhijue he zifa xing [By accident or design: intuition and spontaneity in multiple voice translation]. *Han Feng* (2019): 72–85.

"Recollecting a Moment in Time: Reflections on Dung Kai-cheung's *The Catalog*." *Cha* blog, May 14, 2020. https://chajournal.blog/2020/05/13/the-catalog/.

Miscellaneous Translations in Books and Journals

"Clouds" by Ho Ch'i-fang. Reprinted in *Stand* (Newcastle) 15, no. 3 (1974).

"Three poems from Pi Lin pi Kong zhan ge (1974)." *Modern Chinese Literature Newsletter* 2, no. 2 (Fall 1976): 16–27.

"Let there be trees..." by Li Kuang-t'ien, *Christian Science Monitor* (December 16, 1976) (not refereed).

"Waiting for Rain" by Ho Ch'i-fang. *Modern Chinese Literature Newsletter* 3, no. 2 (Fall 1977): 1–3.

"Postscript to the Reprinting of Family" by Ba Jin. *Modern Chinese Literature Newsletter* (Spring 1978): 13–14.

"Smoke Shadows" by Yu Ta-fu. *Renditions* 9 (Spring 1978): 65–70.

"Sunflowers Bright He Selected" by Zou Difan. *Westerly* no. 3 (September 1981): 32.

"A Posthumous Son" by Ye Shaojun in *A Posthumous Son and other stories*, edited by Bonnie S. McDougall and Lewis S. Robinson. Hong Kong: Commercial Press, 1979. Reprinted in *The Columbia Anthology of Modern Chinese Literature*, edited by Joseph S. M. Lau and Howard Goldblatt. New York: Columbia University Press, 1995, 35–43. Reprinted by Singapore: Asiapac 1987.

"Poems by Ho Ch'i-fang, Ho Ching-chi, Fang Ching-yuan etc." In *The Literature of the People's Republic of China*, edited by Hsu Kai-yu, Bloomington: Indiana University Press, 1980.

"The Sparkling Milky Way" by Fang Mu and "The Paperwork Chief" by Yi Heyuan. In *Modern Chinese Literature Newsletter* 6, no. 1 (Spring 1980): 46–50.

"Two Poems by Cao Changqing." *Modern Chinese Literature Newsletter* 6, no. 2 (Fall 1980): 21

"New Poems from China: Eleven Poems by Bei Dao." In *Modern Chinese Literature Newsletter* 6, no. 2 (Fall 1980): 22–28.

"Three Poems by Gu Cheng." *Modern Chinese Literature Newsletter* 7, nos. 1-2 (1981): 9–12.

"Three Poems by Bei Dao." *Modern Chinese Literature Newsletter* 7, nos. 1-2 (1981): 13–16.

"Varieties of Contemporary Chinese Poetry" (poems by Zou Difan, Feng Jingyuan and Qiu Xiaolong). *Westerly*, Contemporary China Issue (September 1981).

"Voices of Spring." Written by Wang Meng. *Chinese Literature* (1983): 23–36. Reprinted in *Butterfly and other stories*. Beijing: Chinese Literature, 1983.

"Discontent" by Luo Gengye and "Lost Identity," "Thinking of You on New Year's Eve," "Temptation," "Five Sketches of Student Life," "Street Scene" by Qiu Xiaolong. In *Stubborn Weeds: Popular and Controversial Chinese Literature after the Cultural Revolution*, edited by Perry Link. Bloomington: Indiana University Press, 1983.

"Moon on the Manuscript" by Zhao Zhenkai (Bei Dao) and "The Bank," "Tomorrow, No," "Boat Ticket," "The Old Temple," "Chords," "Sleep, Valley," "A Toast," "You Wait on the Rain," "The Host," "Untitled," "For Many Years," "Random Thoughts," "Notes in the Rain," "The Window on the Cliff," and "August Sleepwalker" by Bei Dao. Special Issue on Chinese Literature Today, Renditions nos. 19 & 20 (Spring & Autumn 1983): 173–178, 195–208. Issue reprinted as *Trees on the Mountain: An Anthology of Chinese Writing*, edited by Stephen C. Soong and John Minford. Hong Kong: Chinese University Press, 1984.

"Moon on the Manuscript" by Zhao Zhenkai. Special Issue on Chinese Literature Today, *Renditions*, nos. 19 & 20 (Spring & Autumn 1983): 173–178.

"Chu Hsiang: Thirteen Lyric Poems." Special Issue on Poetry and Poetics, *Renditions*, nos. 21 & 22 (Spring & Autumn 1984): 241–251. Issue reprinted as *A Brotherhood of Song*, ed. Stephen C. Soong and John Minford. Hong Kong: Chinese University Press 1985.

"Bei Dao: Ten Poems." Renditions 23 (Spring 1985): 111–119.

"Thirteen Happiness Street" by Bei Dao. *Renditions*, no. 24 (Autumn 1985): 5–12.

"Open ground" (short story) by Wanzhi (Chen Maiping) and "Poems by Bei Dao." Special issue of the *Bulletin of Concerned Asian Scholars* 16, no. 3 (July–Sept. 1984). Issue reprinted in *Contemporary Chinese Literature: An Anthology of Post-Mao Fiction and Poetry*, edited by Michael S. Duke. New York: Sharpe, 1985. "Open Ground" is on 9–10; "Poems by Bei Dao," 41–46; "Farewell," "The Garland's Soliloquy," and "The Boat from the Distant Past" by Gu Cheng, 49, 50–51; and "Poems by Xie Ye, Jiang Wenyan, and Zhang Zhen," 55–56.

"Lu Li's Six Poems." *Chinese Literature* (Summer 1985): 160–163.

"Poems" by Liu Gangshan et al. *Chinese Literature* (Winter 1985): 145–152.

"Poems by seven women poets (Zheng Min, Wang Erbei, Zheng Ling, Lin Zi, Shu ting, Bai Hong, Wang Xiaoni)." *Chinese Literature* (Spring 1986).

"A Comparison of Chinese and Western Poetry" by Zhu Guangqian. *Chinese Literature* (Summer 1986): 197–208.

"The Masked Dance" by Chen Kaige. *2PLUS2*, no. 5 (1986).

"Thirteen Happiness Street" by Zhao Zhenkai. In *Seeds of Fire: Chinese Voices of Conscience*, edited by Geremie Barmé and John Minford. Hong Kong: Far Eastern Economic Review, 1986. Rev. and expanded ed., New York: Hill and Wang, 1988. Further expanded ed., New York: Farrar and Strauss, 1989.

"The Song," "The First Morning in Vietnam," "Reminiscence," "Do Not Wash Away the Red," and "Sound" by Ho Ch'i-fang. Reprinted in *Twentieth Century Asian Verse*, 4–8. New York: Poetry Anthology Press, 1990.

Two poems both titled "Untitled" by Bei Dao. Reprinted in *Grand Street* 36 (1990): 172–175.

"Temptation" by Qiu Xiaolong, and "The Old Temple" and "Requiem" by Bei Dao. "Temptation" was co-translated with Bei Dao, "The Old Temple" translated by Bonnie S. McDougall, and "Requiem" co-translated with Chen Maiping. Reprinted in *Chinese Poetry Through the Words of the People*, edited by Bonnie McCandless, 123–125. New York: Ballantine Books, 1991.

"A Green World" by Bai Hong and "Silkworms" by Zheng Min. Reprinted in *Women of the Red Plain: an Anthology of Contemporary Chinese Women's Poetry*, edited by Ji Cheng, 20 and 156. London: Penguin Books, 1992.

"Language" by Bei Dao. Reprinted in *On Prejudice: A Global Perspective*, edited by Daniela Gioseffi. New York: Anchor Books, 1993.

"Declaration," "Résumé," and "Another Legend" by Bei Dao. Co-translated with Susan Ternent Cooke. Reprinted in *The Columbia Anthology of Modern Chinese Literature*, edited by Joseph S. M. Lau and Howard Goldblatt, 569–571. New York: Columbia University Press, 1995.

"A Picture," "The August Sleepwalker," and "A Day" by Bei Dao. Reprinted in *The Spaces of Hope: Poetry for our times and places*, edited by Peter Jay, 18, 73, 74–75. London: Anvil Press Poetry, 1998.

"The Answer," "The August Sleepwalker," and "He Opens Wide a Third Eye" by Bei Dao. "He Opens Wide a Third Eye" was co-translated with Chen Maiping. Reprinted in *Poems for the Millennium: The University of California Book of Modern and Postmodern Poetry*. Vol 2, *From Postwar to Millennium*, edited by Jerome Rothenberg and Pierre Joris. Berkeley: University of California Press, 1998.

"Declaration," "Requiem," "A Picture," "Gains," and "The Bell" by Bei Dao. Reprinted in *At the Round Earth's Imagined Corners: A Multicultural Anthology of Contemporary Poetry*, edited by Ken Watson, 1–4. Rozelle: St. Clair Press, 1999.

"Night: Theme and Variations" by Bei Dao. Reprinted in *Approaching Literature in the 21st Century: Fiction, Poetry, Drama*, edited by Peter Schakel and Jack Reid, 774–776. Boston: Bedford/St.Martins, 2005.

"Beijing Sketches" by Leung Ping-kwan. *Renditions* 69 (Spring 2008): 112–123.

"Sugar Street" and "Ice House Street" by Dung Kai-cheung. *Edinburgh Review* 124 (August 2008): 28–31.

"Rainstorm" by Ng Mei-kwan. *Long Paddock* (online edition of *Southerly*), May 2012.

"Irina's Hat" by Tie Ning. In *Irina's Hat: New Short Stories from China*, edited by Josh Stenberg, 263–282. Portland: MerwinAsia, 2012,

"Accomplices," "The Window on the Cliff," "On Tradition," "It has always been so," "The Art of Poetry," "Starting from Yesterday," "SOS," and "A Picture" by Bei Dao. "A Picture" was co-translated with Chen Maiping. In *Jade Ladder: Contemporary Chinese Poetry*, edited by W. N. Herbert and Yang Lian, 55–59. Tarset: Bloodaxe Books, 2012.

"Gray" by Dung Kai-cheung. In *World Literature Today* (November 2015): 14–15.

"My Hopes for the Critics," "On Conducting Ourselves as Fathers Today," and "What Happens After Nora Walks Out." In *Jottings under Lamplight* by Lu Xun, edited by Eileen J. Cheng and Kirk A. Denton, 194–196, 127–139, 256–262. Cambridge: Harvard University Press, 2017.

"Declaration," "The Answer," and "Local Accent" by Bei Dao. In *A Century of Modern Chinese Poetry: An Anthology*, edited by Michelle Yeh, Zhangbin Li, and Frank Stewart, 125–127. Seattle: University of Washington Press, 2023.

Miscellaneous Translations, Co-translated

"Twin Flowers," "The Tiger Tally," "Cai Wenji," and "Wu Zetian" by Guo Moruo. Co-translated with Peng Fumin. In *Selected Works of Guo*

Moruo: Five Historical Plays, 1–86, 193–313, 315–406, 407–521. Beijing: Foreign Languages Press, 1984.

"The Chiming Clock" by Chen Maiping. Co-translated with Kam Louie. *Renditions* 26 (Autumn 1986): 7–10.

"Restructuring the Galaxy," "Evening Scene," "The Time of Frost Descending," "On the Road," "The Bell," and "Requiem" by Bei Dao. Co-translated with Chen Maiping. Reprinted in *New Directions: An International Anthology of Prose and Poetry*, 1–5, 54. New York: New Directions, 1990.

"The Morning's Story," "For Only a Second," " The Collection," "The East's Imagination," "A Bach Concert," "Notes on Reading," "Gains," "Coming Home at Night," "April," and "Discovery" by Bei Dao. Co-translated with Chen Maiping. Reprinted in *The Manhattan Review* 5, no. 2 (Fall 1990): 4–12.

"A Day," "A Country Night," "Night: Theme and Variations," "In a Decade," "Declaration," "Nightmare," "The Old Temple," "Coming Home at Night," "The Morning's Story," and "Requiem" by Bei Dao. Co-translated with Chen Maiping. Reprinted in *Out of the Howling Storm: The New Chinese Poetry*, edited by Tony Barnstone, 41–48. Hanover: University Press of New England, 1993. "Requiem" reprinted in *Chicago Review* 39, nos. 3 & 4 (1993): 288.

"Prague," "He Opens Wide a Third Eye," "Along the Way," and "At This Moment" by Bei Dao. Co-translated with Chen Maiping. Reprinted in *Under-sky Underground: Chinese Writing Today 1*, edited by Henry Y. H. Zhao and John Cayley, 51–54. London: Wellsweep Press, 1994.

"Mystery," "Sand," and "In the Distance, Snow" by Wan Zhi [Chen Maiping]. Co-translated with Kam Louie. *Renditions* 52 (Autumn 1999): 45–70.

"Spring Garden Lane" by Dong Kai Cheung. Co-translated with Wong Nim Yan. *Renditions* 66 (Autumn 2006): 111–113.

"*Dear Husband*" by Ding Xilin. Co-translated with Flora Lam. *Renditions* 69 (Spring 2008): 62–75.

"The Bowl" by Xi Xi. Co-translated with Wong Nim Yan. *Renditions* 69 (Spring 2008): 103–106.

"*The Cold and The Dark*: extracts" by Pu Songling. Co-translated with C. D. Alison Bailey. *Renditions* 70 (Autumn 2008): 65–88.

Bibliography

Austen, Jane. *Pride and Prejudice*. Illustrations by Rhys Williams. Sydney: Dymock's Book Arcade, 1949.

Barmé, Geremie, and John Minford, eds. *Seeds of Fire: Chinese Voices of Conscience*. Hong Kong: Far Eastern Economic Review, 1986.

Butt, Rashid. "My Days in China," in *Living in China by Twenty Authors from Abroad* Beijing: New World Press, 1978.

Byatt, A. S. *The Shadow of the Sun: A Novel*. London: Vintage, 1991.

Cheng, Eileen J., and Kirk A. Denton, eds. *Jottings under Lamplight*. Cambridge, MA: Harvard University Press, 2017.

Hanan, Patrick. "The Technique of Lu Hsun's Fiction." *Harvard Journal of Asiatic Studies* 34 (1974). Reprinted in Hanan, *Chinese Fiction of the Nineteenth and Early Twentieth Centuries: Essays*. New York: Columbia University Press, 2004.

Hsia, Tsi-an. "Twenty Years After the Yenan Forum." In *The Gate of Darkness: Studies on the Leftist Literary Movement in China*, edited by Tsi-an Hsia, 234–263. Seattle: University of Washington Press, 1968.

Hsu Kai-yu. *The Literature of the People's Republic of China*. Bloomington: Indiana University Press, 1989.

Kwan, Uganda Sze Pui. "Strategizing Hong Kong Literature in the World: Self-collaborative Translation of Dung Kai Cheung's *Atlas*." In *A Century of Chinese Literature in Translation (1919–2019): English Publication and Reception*, edited by Leah Gerber and Lintao Qi, 116–131. London: Routledge, 2020.

Li Yi 李翼. "Dao bu li qi, yi lun jian bei: Audaliya hanxuejia Du Boni jiaoshou fangtanlu' 道不离器，译论兼备———澳大利亚汉学家杜博妮教授访谈录 [The Tao is inseparable from the instrument and has both translation and theory: an interview with Australian sinologist Professor Bonnie S. McDougall], *School of Foreign Languages, Shanghai Jiaotong University* 38, no. 2 (March 2017).

———. "Du Boni fanyi yanjiu: wenti yu qianjing" 杜博妮翻译研究: 问题与前景 [Review of research on Bonnie S. McDougall: Problems and prospects], *Waiyu jiaoxue* 外语教学.

———. "Jiyu yuliaoku de "Qi wang" Ying yiben fanyi fengge bijiao yanjiu" 基于语料库的《棋王》英译本翻译风格比较研究 [A corpus-based comparative study of the text corpus in the English translation of "The Chess King"]. *Shandong Foreign Language Teaching* 41, no. 1 (2020).

———. "Zai Hanxue yu fanyi zhi jian: Audaliya Hanxuejia Du Boni de Zhongguo xiandangdai wenxue fanyi yanjiu' 在汉学与翻译之间——澳大利亚汉学家杜博妮的中国现当代文学翻译研究 [Between sinology and translation——Australian Bonnie S. McDougall's translation studies on modern and contemporary Chinese literature].

Li Ziyun 李子雲. "Huashuo Ah Cheng" 話說阿城, in *Jiushi niandai yuekan* 九十年代月刊 (June 1986): 92–93.

Mao Zedong, *Mō Takutō shū* 毛泽东集 [Collected writings of Mao Zedong]. 10 vols. Tokyo: Hokubō sha, 1970–1972.

Powell, Anthony. *Hearing Secret Harmonies*. Vol. 12, *A Dance to the Music of Time*. London: Flamingo, 1983. First published in 1975.

Qiao, Geng. "Gift-giving: Panda Books Series and Chinese literature 'Walking toward the World.'" In *A Century of Chinese Literature in Translation (1919–2019): English Publication and Reception*, edited by Leah Gerber and Lintao Qi, 57–70. London: Routledge, 2020.

Schram, Stuart. *Mao's Road to Power: Revolutionary Writings 1912–1949*. Vol. 8. New York: M. E. Sharpe, 2014.

Snow, Edward. *Living China*. London: Harrup, 1936.

Spence, Jonathan. "Forever Jade," *New York Review of Books*, April 17, 1980.

Wan Zhi 萬之 [Chen Maiping 陳邁平]. "Ju san li he, dou yi cheng liu shui luo hua: zhuiji "Jintian" haiwai fukan chuqi de jici bianwei huiyi" 聚散離合,都已成流水落花：追記 "今天'海外複刊的幾次編委會議" [Gathered, they scattered; the divided now join; all become rivers in stream and blossoms in fall: retrospective notes on the editorial meetings of *Today's* overseas edition], *Jintian* [Today] 100 (Spring 2013): 1–24.

Wang Shiqing. *Lu Xun: A Biography.* Beijing: Foreign Languages Press, 1984.

Wechsler, Robert. *Performing Without a Stage: The Art of Literary Translation.* North Haven: Catbird Press, 1998.

Wilding, Michael. "Adventurous Spirits." In *UQP: The Writer's Press 1948–1998*, edited by Craig Munro, 84–100. St. Lucia: University of Queensland Press, 1998.

About the Author

Bonnie S. McDougall (FAHA) is Honorary Professor at the School of Languages and Cultures at the University of Sydney, Emeritus Fellow at the Australian Academy of the Humanities, Emeritus Professor of Chinese at the University of Edinburgh, and Honorary Fellow at the Australian Society for Humanities. The most recent additions to Dr. McDougall's extensive list of publications include *Translation Zones in Modern China: Authoritarian Command Versus Gift Exchange* as well as co-translations with Anders Hansson: *Atlas: The Archeology of an Imaginary City* by Dung Kai-cheung (Columbia University Press), *Cantonese Love Stories: Twenty-five Vignettes of a City* by Dung Kai-cheung (Penguin Special), and *A Catalog of Such Stuff as Dreams Are Made On* by Dung Kai-cheung (Columbia University Press).

Cambria Sinophone Translation Series

General Editor: Kyle Shernuk (Georgetown University)
Advisor: Christopher Lupke (University of Alberta)

The members of the editorial board are:

- John Balcom (Middlebury Institute of International Studies)
- Mark Bender (The Ohio State University)
- Michael Berry (UCLA)
- Chan Cheow Thia (National University of Singapore)
- Jannis Jizhou Chen (CUHK)
- Howard Chiang (UC Davis)
- Kuei-fen Chiu (National Chung Hsing University)
- Chih-wei Chung (Fu Jen Catholic University, Taiwan)
- Howard Goldblatt (University of Notre Dame)
- Hsin-Chin Evelyn Hsieh (National Taiwan University)
- Dingru Huang (Tufts University)
- Theodore Huters (UCLA)
- Wilt Idema (Harvard University)
- Mabel Lee (University of Sydney)
- Yu-lin Lee (Academia Sinica)
- Sebastian Hsien-hao Liao (National Taiwan University)
- Pei-yin Lin (University of Hong Kong)

- Sylvia Li-chun Lin (University of Notre Dame)
- Victor Mair (University of Pennsylvania)
- Bonnie McDougall (University of Sydney)
- Mei Chia-ling (National Taiwan University)
- David Der-wei Wang (Harvard University)
- Frances Weightman (University of Leeds)

Books in the Cambria Sinophone Translation Series

Contemporary Taiwanese Women Writers: An Anthology edited by Jonathan Stalling, Lin Tai-man, and Yanwing Leung

Painting History: China's Revolution in a Global Context by Jiawei Shen, translated and edited by Mabel Lee

Mo Yan Speaks: Lectures and Speeches by the Nobel Laureate from China by Mo Yan, translated and edited by Shiyan Xu

Strange Bedfellows [*Chi gua shidai de ernumen* 吃瓜时代的儿女们] by Liu Zhenyun, translated by Howard Goldblatt and Sylvia Li-chun Lin

From Rural China to the Ivy League: Reminiscences of Transformations in Modern Chinese History by Yü Ying-shih, translated by Josephine Chiu-Duke and Michael S. Duke

Calling for a New Renaissance by Gao Xingjian, translated by Mabel Lee and Yan Qian

Urban Scenes by Liu Na'ou, introduced and translated by Yaohua Shi and Judith M. Amory

Translation Stories from Modern China by Bonnie S. McDougall

www.ingramcontent.com/pod-product-compliance
Lightning Source LLC
Chambersburg PA
CBHW071404300426
44114CB00016B/2181